DAY HIKES IN
SEQUOIA AND
KINGS CANYON
NATIONAL PARKS

by Robert Stone

Day Hike Books, Inc.
RED LODGE, MONTANA

Published by Day Hike Books, Inc.
P.O. Box 865
Red Lodge, Montana 59068

Distributed by The Globe Pequot Press
246 Goose Lane
P.O. Box 480
Guilford, CT 06437-0480
800-243-0495 (direct order) · 800-820-2329 (fax order)
www.globe-pequot.com

Photographs by Robert Stone
Design by Paula Doherty

The author has made every attempt to provide accurate
information in this book. However, trail routes and features may
change—please use common sense and forethought, and be mindful
of your own capabilities. Let this book guide you, but be aware
that each hiker assumes responsibility for their own safety.
The author and publisher do not assume any responsibility for loss,
damage or injury caused through the use of this book.

Cover photo: Huckleberry Meadow—Alta Trail Loop, Hike 38
Back cover photo: Trail of the Sequoias, Hike 35

Table of Contents

Redwood Canyon

Stony Creek to Lodgepole and Wolverton

Giant Forest

The Foothills to Ash Mountain Entrance

Mineral King

About the Hikes
Sequoia and Kings Canyon National Parks

Sequoia National Park and Kings Canyon National Park are located at the southern end of the 400-mile long Sierra Nevada Mountain Range, the largest single mountain range in the United States. The two parks are adjacent, without noticeable boundaries, and are managed as a single entity. The scenic 46-mile Generals Highway connects the two national parks, but the vast majority of the area is without roads. There is no road access from the east and ninety percent of the back-country is designated wilderness.

The Generals Highway begins in Sequoia at the Ash Mountain entrance by the town of Three Rivers. The twisting roadway climbs steeply from the arid foothills to the Giant Forest plateau while gaining nearly 5,000 feet in only 16 miles. The road continues to Grant Grove in Kings Canyon, crossing Big Baldy Saddle, the high point of the road at 7,643 feet. Kings Canyon Highway (Highway 180) and Mineral King Road extend to the east from the Generals Highway, offering access into the heart of these incredible canyons.

The vegetation, wildlife and climate in the parks are varied and diverse. The elevations range from 1,300 feet, at the east end of the San Joaquin Valley in the western foothills of the Sierra slope, to 14,495 feet in the High Sierra at Mount Whitney, the highest point in the contiguous United States. The ecological zones range from Mediterranean dry scrub forests with brush and oak to the arctic grandeur of the towering snow-capped peaks along the crest of the High Sierra, where the Great Western Divide lies. Within Sequoia and Kings Canyon are the headwaters of four major California rivers—the Kaweah, Kern, Kings and San Joaquin.

Kings Canyon National Park has two hubs with varying scenery—Cedar Grove and Grant Grove. Cedar Grove sits at the bottom of Kings Canyon alongside the South Fork Kings River. This 8,200-foot deep chasm is the deepest canyon in North America. It is 2000 feet deeper than the Grand Canyon. The sheer granite walls and peaks rise nearly a mile above the glacially carved U-shaped canyon. Hikes lead up the canyon walls to phenomenal views.

Grant Grove is located in a shady, moist forested area and is surrounded by spectacular groves of behemoth sequoias, including Redwood Mountain, the world's largest giant sequoia grove. Hikes range from secluded sequoia groves to ridgetop trails with views extending to the Great Western Divide on the east and the coastal ranges on the west.

Sequoia National Park is primarily known for the stunning giant sequoias, *Sequoiadendron giganteum,* the largest living things on earth. The beautiful and impressive Giant Forest, named by John Muir, encompasses five square miles with more than 40 miles of hiking paths. The interconnecting network of trails weave through magnificent stands of giant sequoias and a half dozen major meadows. Several other sequoia groves are found throughout the two parks.

Human occupation from the past is also present in the park. There are various pioneer cabins built inside fallen, hollowed-out sequoias, as well as enormous sequoia stumps, remnants from the logging area. There are old Indian village sites with bedrock mortars, holes carved into granite slabs by Indians preparing meals, and various pictographs.

On the edge of the Giant Forest Plateau, Moro Rock, a large granite dome, towers over the immense Middle Fork Kaweah River canyon. From the hike atop this monolith are tremendous views of the serrated, snow-capped summits of the Great Western Divide to the east and the San Joaquin Valley basin to the west.

Mineral King joined Sequoia National Park in 1978. As the name implies, the Mineral King area was once inundated by optimistic miners in the 1870s. The hikes in this alpine valley are surrounded by towering peaks and pristine wilderness. A steep, narrow, winding road leads into the glacially sculpted high-mountain valley beneath the knobby peaks of the Great Western Divide.

The hikes in this guide are divided into six distinct regions, taking you to 61 of the best day hikes and sights along the western side of these national parks. Each hike is designed to get you to the trailhead and onto the trail with clear, concise directions. To help you decide which hikes are most appealing to you, a summary of the highlights is included with each hike.

These hikes are found within a short distance of Generals Highway, Highway 180 or Mineral King Road. An overall map of the two national parks and the hikes can be found on the next page. Additional area maps are found throughout the book as well as an individual map for each hike. The U.S.G.S. maps and other supplementary maps listed with the hikes are not necessary unless extending your hike further into the backcountry. (Wilderness permits are required for overnight trips, as well as experience, maps, proper clothing and equipment, and common sense. Check with visitor centers and ranger stations for more information.)

From the north end of Kings Canyon to the southern end of Sequoia, the best way to discover these incredible national parks is on foot. These hikes will introduce you to the world's largest trees and some of the most impressive canyons, rock formations and scenery found anywhere.

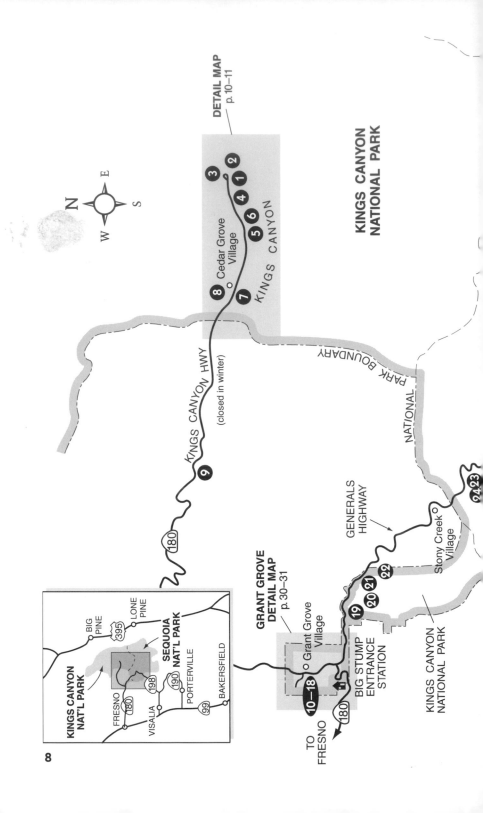

DETAIL MAP
p. 10–11

KINGS CANYON NATIONAL PARK

Cedar Grove Village

KINGS CANYON

N
W   E
S

KINGS CANYON HWY
(closed in winter)

PARK BOUNDARY

NATIONAL

KINGS CANYON NAT'L PARK

SEQUOIA NAT'L PARK

BIG PINE

LONE PINE

FRESNO
VISALIA
PORTERVILLE
BAKERSFIELD

395
180
198
190
99

GENERALS HIGHWAY

Stony Creek Village

GRANT GROVE DETAIL MAP
p. 30–31

Grant Grove Village

BIG STUMP ENTRANCE STATION

KINGS CANYON NATIONAL PARK

TO FRESNO

180

180

10–18

19

20 21
22

23 24

9

1 2
3
4
5 6
7
8

8

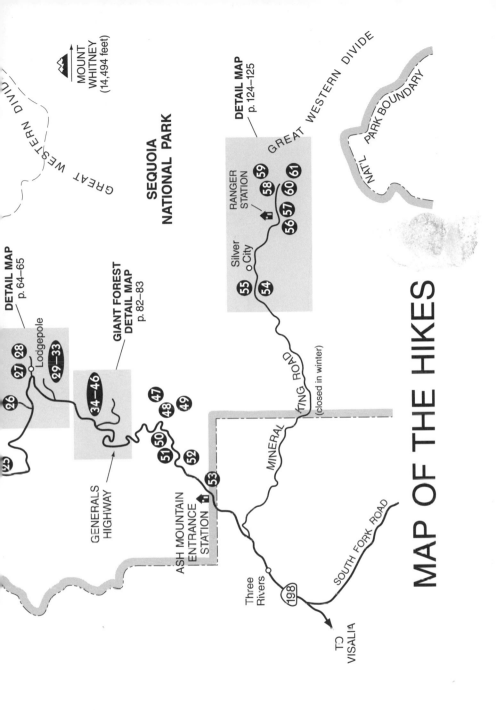

MAP OF THE HIKES

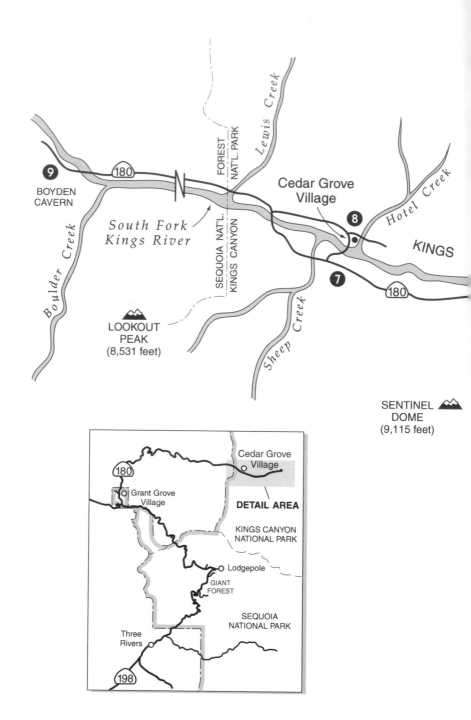

9
BOYDEN
CAVERN

180

South Fork
Kings River

Boulder Creek

Lewis Creek

FOREST
NAT'L. PARK

SEQUOIA NAT'L.
KINGS CANYON

Cedar Grove
Village

Hotel Creek

8

KINGS

7

180

Sheep Creek

LOOKOUT
PEAK
(8,531 feet)

SENTINEL
DOME
(9,115 feet)

180

Cedar Grove
Village

Grant Grove
Village

DETAIL AREA

KINGS CANYON
NATIONAL PARK

Lodgepole

GIANT
FOREST

SEQUOIA
NATIONAL PARK

Three
Rivers

198

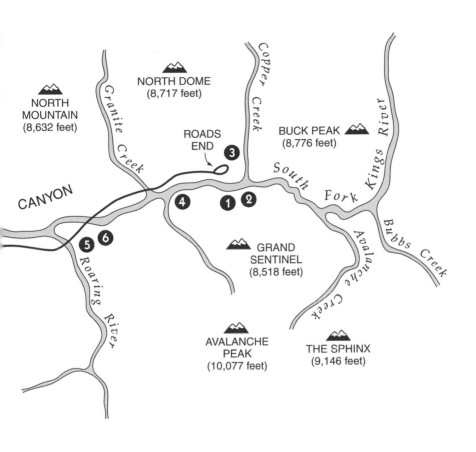

NORTH DOME
(8,717 feet)

NORTH
MOUNTAIN
(8,632 feet)

Copper Creek

Granite Creek

ROADS
END
3

BUCK PEAK
(8,776 feet)

Kings River

South Fork

CANYON

4 **1** **2**

5 **6**

GRAND
SENTINEL
(8,518 feet)

Roaring River

Avalanche Creek

Bubbs Creek

AVALANCHE
PEAK
(10,077 feet)

THE SPHINX
(9,146 feet)

N
W — E
S

KINGS CANYON
HIKES 1–9

Hike 1
Bubbs Creek

Hiking distance: 4.5 mile loop
Hiking time: 2 hours
Elevation gain: 70 feet
Maps: U.S.G.S. The Sphinx
        Sequoia Natural History Association—Cedar Grove

Summary of hike: The trail to Bubbs Creek parallels the South Fork of the Kings River with views of towering, glacially carved peaks on every side. Grand Sentinel and The Sphinx are on the south canyon wall, North Dome and Buck Peak on the north wall and Glacier Monument rises in the east. The hike heads up Kings Canyon along the south side of the river valley to the Bubbs Creek Bridge and returns along the north bank. The loop trail includes four bridge crossings. This hike is the first portion of Hike 2 to Mist Falls.

Driving directions: From Cedar Grove Village, drive 0.2 miles to the main road (Highway 180). Turn left (east) and continue 5.4 miles to the south end of the parking lot on the right at the Roads End loop.

Hiking directions: The trailhead is at the beginning of the parking loop. Head south to a bridge crossing the South Fork Kings River. After crossing, bear left upstream. Continue past large boulders, parallel to the South Fork Kings River, and up the valley between the towering peaks. Cross meadows dotted with ponderosa pine and cedar trees to Avalanche Creek. A short distance ahead is a signed junction. Straight ahead is a log bridge crossing Bubbs Creek. After viewing the cascades, return to the junction, and take the north trail across Bailey Bridge at the confluence of Bubbs Creek and the Kings River. After crossing is a junction. The right fork leads to Mist Falls (Hike 2). The left fork is the return trail for this hike along the north side of the river. Near the trailhead, cross a wooden bridge over Copper Creek, returning to the parking lot.

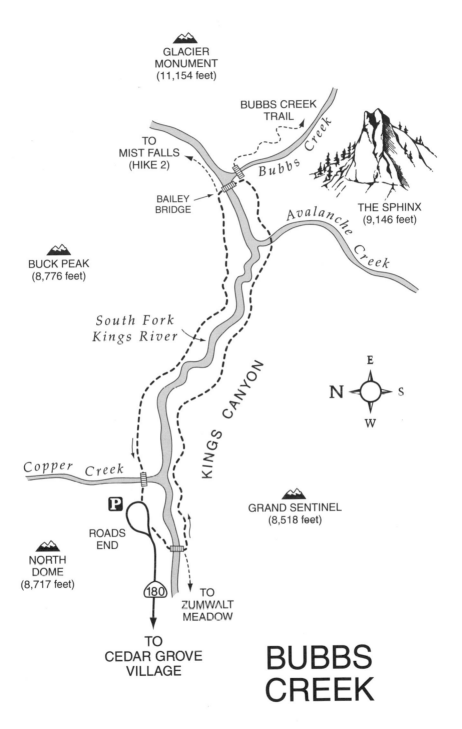

GLACIER
MONUMENT
(11,154 feet)

BUBBS CREEK
TRAIL

Bubbs Creek

TO
MIST FALLS
(HIKE 2)

BAILEY
BRIDGE

THE SPHINX
(9,146 feet)

Avalanche Creek

BUCK PEAK
(8,776 feet)

*South Fork
Kings River*

KINGS CANYON

N • E • S • W

Copper Creek

GRAND SENTINEL
(8,518 feet)

P

ROADS
END

NORTH
DOME
(8,717 feet)

180

TO
ZUMWALT
MEADOW

TO
CEDAR GROVE
VILLAGE

BUBBS
CREEK

Hike 2
Mist Falls

Hiking distance: 8.5 miles round trip
Hiking time: 4 hours
Elevation gain: 650 feet
Maps: U.S.G.S. The Sphinx
        Sequoia Natural History Association—Cedar Grove

Summary of hike: Mist Falls drops 50 feet over a wide granite ledge into a pool lined with boulders. Huge, flat rocks 100 feet below the falls are perfect spots to view the waterfall. The trail parallels the South Fork Kings River along the valley floor between towering canyon walls for the first 2.5 miles. The last two miles head up the narrow canyon into Paradise Valley past numerous cascades and cataracts.

Driving directions: From Cedar Grove Village, drive 0.2 miles to the main road (Highway 180). Turn left (east) and continue 5.4 miles to the south end of the parking lot on the right at the Roads End loop.

Hiking directions: Follow the hiking directions for Hike 1 to Bailey Bridge and the junction at 2.5 miles. The left fork is the return route for this hike. Take the right fork to Mist Falls—the Paradise Valley Trail. Head up the narrow, steep-walled canyon, curving around the east side of Buck Peak. Continue parallel to the South Fork Kings River. The first mile is fairly level, while the second mile heads steadily uphill. At 4 miles, the trail passes a dramatic series of cascades, cataracts and pools. The trail reaches the Mist Falls junction at 4.5 miles. The left fork leads to Paradise Valley, 3 miles further. Take the right fork, leaving the main trail, down to the base of Mist Falls. There are large boulders to sit on and view the powerful falls. To return, head down the canyon back to Bailey Bridge. Take the right fork along the north side of the river. Cross the footbridge over Copper Creek, returning to the parking lot.

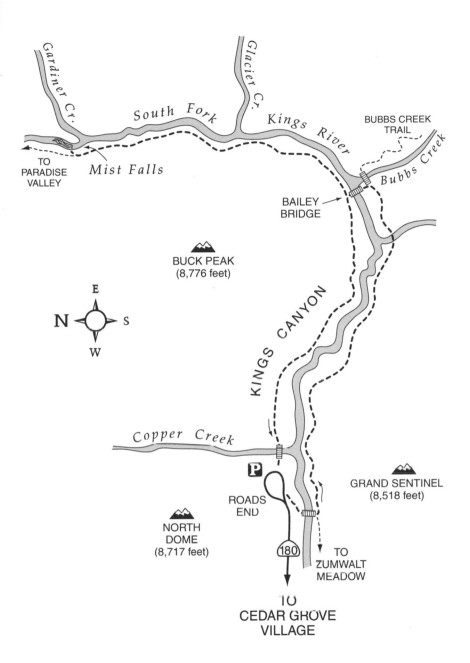

MIST FALLS

Hike 3
Copper Creek Trail to Overlook

Hiking distance: 3 miles round trip
Hiking time: 1.5 hours
Elevation gain: 1,350 feet
Maps: U.S.G.S. The Sphinx
        Sequoia Natural History Association—Cedar Grove

Summary of hike: The Copper Creek Trail heads strenuously up the north wall of Kings Canyon between North Dome and Buck Peak. It leads to Lower Tent Meadow, a backpacker campground, and on to the Monarch Divide. The trail offers views of Copper Creek flowing through the deep, narrow side canyon. This hike ends at a magnificent overlook of Kings Canyon, 1.5 miles from the trailhead.

Driving directions: From Cedar Grove Village, drive 0.2 miles to the main road (Highway 180). Turn left (east) and continue 5.6 miles to the far end of the parking lot at the north end of the Roads End loop.

Hiking directions: Head north past the trailhead sign, and begin climbing the eastern flank of North Dome on the open exposed slopes. Each switchback on the steep, unrelenting trail gives a better view up and down the forested glacial valley. Across the canyon are great views of Avalanche Peak, The Sphinx and Grand Sentinel. At the end of the switchbacks, the trail leaves Kings Canyon and enters narrow Copper Canyon. This is a good turnaround area.

To hike further, the trail continues to Lower Tent Meadow 2.5 miles ahead.

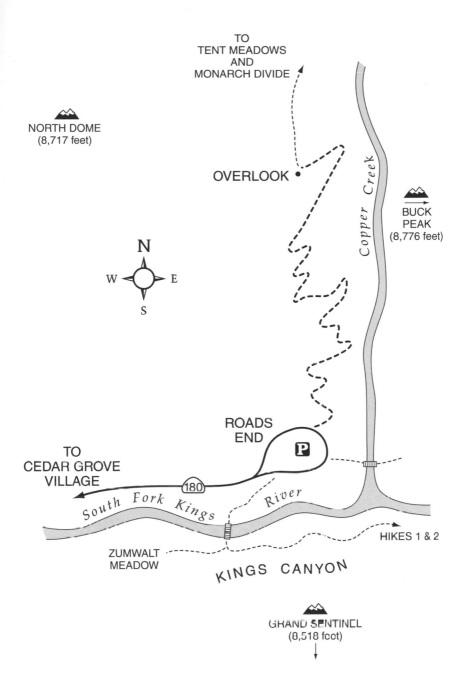

TO
TENT MEADOWS
AND
MONARCH DIVIDE

NORTH DOME
(8,717 feet)

OVERLOOK

Copper Creek

BUCK
PEAK
(8,776 feet)

N
W E
S

ROADS
END

P

TO
CEDAR GROVE
VILLAGE

180

South Fork Kings   River

HIKES 1 & 2

ZUMWALT
MEADOW

KINGS CANYON

GRAND SENTINEL
(8,518 feet)

COPPER CREEK TRAIL

Hike 4
Zumwalt Meadow Trail

Hiking distance: 1.5 mile loop
Hiking time: 1 hour
Elevation gain: 50 feet
Maps: U.S.G.S. The Sphinx
         Sequoia Natural History Association—Cedar Grove

Summary of hike: Zumwalt Meadow is a lush, verdant meadow along the banks of the South Fork Kings River. The trail circles the perimeter of the meadow, from the talus slope of fractured rocks above the meadow to the moist, marshy forest canopy. Two granite monoliths, North Dome and Grand Sentinel, tower above the steep canyon.

Driving directions: From Cedar Grove Village, drive 0.2 miles to the main road (Highway 180). Turn left (east) and continue 4.5 miles towards Roads End to the Zumwalt Meadow parking lot on the right.

Hiking directions: The Zumwalt Nature Trail begins along the banks of the South Fork Kings River. Bear right past the trailhead sign, heading downstream to the suspension bridge crossing the river. After crossing is a junction. The right fork is the River Trail (Hike 6) leading to Roaring River Falls. Take the left fork east towards Zumwalt Meadow. A short distance ahead, by interpretive station #7, is a junction and the beginning of the loop. Take the right fork, the upper trail, through the forest and the talus slopes above the meadow. At the east end of the meadow is another junction. Take the left fork to the river's edge. Return through the meadow parallel to the river. A portion of the trail is on a wooden boardwalk protecting the fragile vegetation. Return to the trailhead across the suspension bridge.

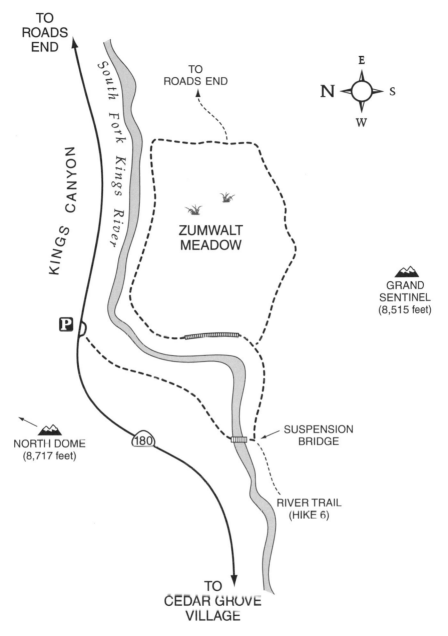

TO
ROADS
END

South Fork Kings River

KINGS CANYON

TO
ROADS END

N — E / S / W (compass)

ZUMWALT
MEADOW

GRAND
SENTINEL
(8,515 feet)

P

NORTH DOME
(8,717 feet)

(180)

SUSPENSION
BRIDGE

RIVER TRAIL
(HIKE 6)

TO
CEDAR GROVE
VILLAGE

ZUMWALT MEADOW
TRAIL

Hike 5
Roaring River Falls

Hiking distance: 1 mile round trip
Hiking time: 30 minutes
Elevation gain: Level
Maps: U.S.G.S. The Sphinx
      Sequoia Natural History Association—Cedar Grove

Summary of hike: Roaring River Falls is a full-bodied, two-tiered 60-foot waterfall. The river catapults over a narrow granite gorge into a deep, wide rock-lined pool. From the viewing areas, only the lower 40 feet of the falls is visible. There are two trails to Roaring River Falls, and both trails are a half-mile round trip. From the east side of Roaring River is a paved, wheelchair accessible trail to a viewpoint. From the west side is a single track trail to an overlook.

Driving directions: From Cedar Grove Village, drive 0.2 miles to the main road (Highway 180). Turn left (east) and continue 3 miles towards Roads End to the Roaring River Falls parking lot on the right. The parking lot is just beyond the bridge crossing over Roaring River.

Hiking directions: Head south past the trailhead sign on the paved path. Granite boulders line the forested trail. Continue past the junction with the River Trail to Zumwalt Meadow on the left (Hike 6). A short distance ahead is the short but powerful Roaring River Falls and a viewing area.

The second access to Roaring River Falls has a view of the falls from the west side of Roaring River. From the parking lot, walk west on the road across the bridge. The well-defined, unpaved path begins 30 yards west of the bridge by a parking pullout. Hike south through the forest, heading upstream for a quarter mile to an overlook of the falls from above the pool.

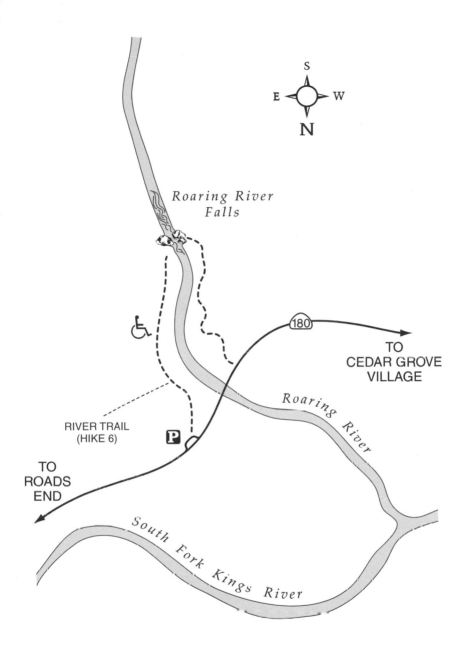

S
E — ⊕ — W
N

Roaring River Falls

180

TO
CEDAR GROVE
VILLAGE

Roaring River

♿

RIVER TRAIL
(HIKE 6)

P

TO
ROADS
END

South Fork Kings River

ROARING RIVER
FALLS

Hike 6
River Trail

Hiking distance: 3.5 miles round trip
Hiking time: 2 hours
Elevation gain: 60 feet
Maps: U.S.G.S. The Sphinx
Sequoia Natural History Association—Cedar Grove

Summary of hike: The River Trail connects the Roaring River Falls Trail (Hike 5) with the Zumwalt Meadow Trail (Hike 4). The trail heads up the forested valley floor parallel to the South Fork of Kings River. North Dome towers to the north while Grand Sentinel looms to the south.

Driving directions: From Cedar Grove Village, drive 0.2 miles to the main road (Highway 180). Turn left (east) and continue 3 miles towards Roads End to the Roaring River Falls parking lot on the right. The parking lot is just beyond the bridge crossing over Roaring River.

Hiking directions: Head south on the paved trail towards Roaring River Falls (Hike 5). Thirty yards short of the waterfall is a signed junction. Take this trail to the left towards Zumwalt Meadow. The first portion of the trail is near the highway. Continue through a forest of cedar, oak and pines. At a half mile, the trail climbs over a moraine, then meets and parallels the South Fork of the Kings River. Continue to a junction at 1.6 miles on the west edge of Zumwalt Meadow by the metal suspension bridge on the left. This is our turnaround spot. Return to the Roaring River along the same trail.

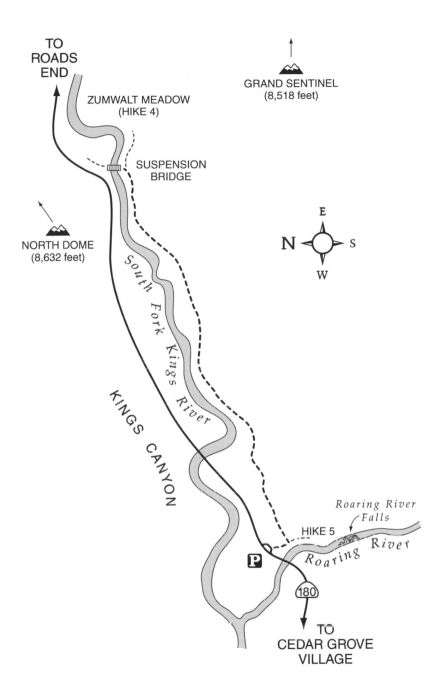

TO
ROADS
END

ZUMWALT MEADOW
(HIKE 4)

GRAND SENTINEL
(8,518 feet)

SUSPENSION
BRIDGE

NORTH DOME
(8,632 feet)

South Fork Kings River

E
N ◇ S
W

KINGS CANYON

Roaring River Falls

HIKE 5

Roaring River

P

180

TO
CEDAR GROVE
VILLAGE

RIVER TRAIL

Hike 7
Don Cecil Trail to Sheep Creek Cascades

Hiking distance: 2 miles round trip
Hiking time: 1 hour
Elevation gain: 600 feet
Maps: U.S.G.S. Cedar Grove
      Sequoia Natural History Association—Cedar Grove

Summary of hike: The Don Cecil Trail climbs six miles up the north-facing slopes of Kings Canyon to Lookout Peak. This hike heads up to Sheep Creek, serving as the water supply for Cedar Grove Village. The trail crosses Sheep Creek in a deep gorge by a series of cascades, fern-lined pools and a wooden bridge crossing. The 11,000-foot peaks of the Monarch Divide can be seen across Kings Canyon to the north.

Driving directions: From Cedar Grove Village, drive 0.2 miles to the main road (Highway 180). Turn left (east) and continue 50 yards to the parking pullout on the left. The trailhead is across the road. From Cedar Grove Village, it is a short walk to the trailhead.

Hiking directions: From the parking pullout, walk east 70 yards along the road to the signed trailhead on the right. Head south on the forested path, and begin ascending the valley wall. At 0.4 miles, the trail crosses an unpaved service road. After crossing, pick up the trail again, and continue traversing the mountainside to an overlook at one mile. From the overlook are views north across Kings Canyon to the snow-tipped peaks of the Monarch Divide in the distance. The trail descends a short distance in the Sheep Creek drainage to a grotto at Sheep Creek. Beautiful whitewater cascades over smooth granite rock into pools. A wooden bridge crosses the creek, the turnaround point for this hike.

To hike further, the trail continues an additional 5 miles and 3,300 feet higher to Lookout Peak at 8,531 feet.

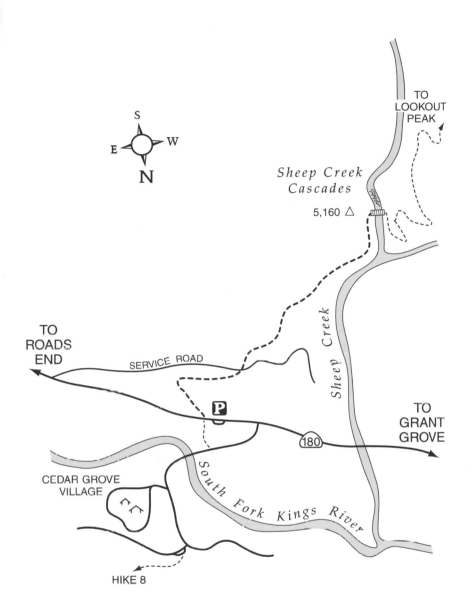

DON CECIL TRAIL
TO THE
SHEEP CREEK CASCADES

Hike 8
Hotel Creek Trail
to Cedar Grove Overlook

Hiking distance: 5 miles round trip
Hiking time: 2.5 hours
Elevation gain: 1,300 feet
Maps: U.S.G.S. Cedar Grove
Sequoia Natural History Association—Cedar Grove

Summary of hike: The Hotel Creek Trail climbs the south-facing wall of Kings Canyon up the open, exposed slope. The trail switches back and forth, climbing steeply from the forested canyon floor. The short switchbacks gain 1,200 feet in 2.5 miles to unobstructed views at the Cedar Grove Overlook. The snow-capped peaks of the Monarch Divide can be seen in the north and the length of Kings Canyon to the south. This route can also be hiked as an 8-mile loop with the Lewis Creek Trail.

Driving directions: From Cedar Grove Village, drive or walk north, following the signs towards the pack station 0.2 miles to the Hotel Creek Trail parking lot on the left.

Hiking directions: Two trails begin at the trailhead. The Lewis Creek Trail heads left. Take the Hotel Creek Trail to the right through the forest of oaks, pines and manzanita. Near the east point of the first switchback is a short side trail, a stock route bearing right down to the cascades at Hotel Creek. Return to the main trail, and continue up many switchbacks to great views of Avalanche Peak, Sentinel Ridge, Sentinel Dome, Lookout Peak, the Sheep Creek drainage, the Roaring River drainage and the glacier-carved Kings Canyon. Near the top, the trail levels off on the bench and traverses the mountainside to the west. At 2 miles is a ridge and a signed trail split. The right fork leads to the Lewis Creek Trail junction. Take the left fork, descending towards the overlook. Gently climb up the rocky ridge to the Cedar Grove Overlook. After tarrying, return on the same trail.

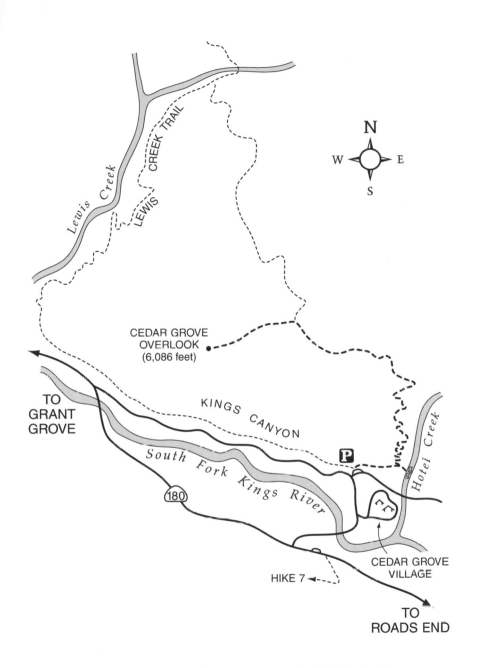

HOTEL CREEK TRAIL

Hike 9
Windy Cliffs Trail to Boulder Creek

Hiking distance: 3 miles round trip
Hiking time: 1.5 hours
Elevation gain: 300 feet
Maps: U.S.G.S. Wren Peak

Summary of hike: The Windy Cliffs Trail traverses the mountainside along a narrow shelf in Kings Canyon high above the South Fork of the Kings River. The trail heads into the steep-walled Boulder Creek Canyon. Boulder Creek cascades down the narrow side canyon, forming numerous deep pools. The trail ends at the creek by steep, rugged rock formations and the remnants of an old bridge.

Driving directions: The trailhead begins by Boydon Cavern, where the bridge crosses over the South Fork Kings River. From Cedar Grove Village, drive 0.2 miles to the main road (Highway 180). Turn right (west) and continue 9.5 miles west to the parking lot on the right across the highway from Boyden Cavern.

From Grant Grove Village, drive 19.4 miles northbound on Highway 180 to the parking lot on the left.

Hiking directions: Cross the highway to the Boyden Cavern parking lot. Take the paved path towards the cave entrance. Head uphill a short distance to a switchback. The switchback leads to the caves. Take the unsigned Windy Cliff Trail straight ahead, heading east past a metal gate on the rocky ledge. The trail curves south and crosses Windy Gulch past magnificent marble cliffs and formations. The path parallels the South Fork of the river from high above. Continue along the ridge, traversing the mountain. At one mile, the trail leaves the Kings River and curves up Boulder Creek Canyon. As you enter the narrow canyon, the trail overlooks the deep pools and cascades of Boulder Creek and gradually descends toward the creek. At 1.5 miles, the trail ends at the creek by rock formations and the remains of a bridge. Return by retracing your steps.

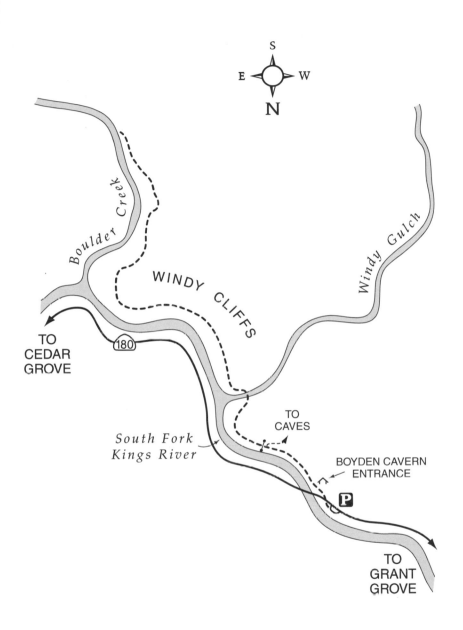

S
E ✦ W
N

Boulder Creek

WINDY CLIFFS

Windy Gulch

TO
CEDAR
GROVE

180

*South Fork
Kings River*

TO
CAVES

BOYDEN CAVERN
ENTRANCE

P

TO
GRANT
GROVE

WINDY CLIFFS TRAIL

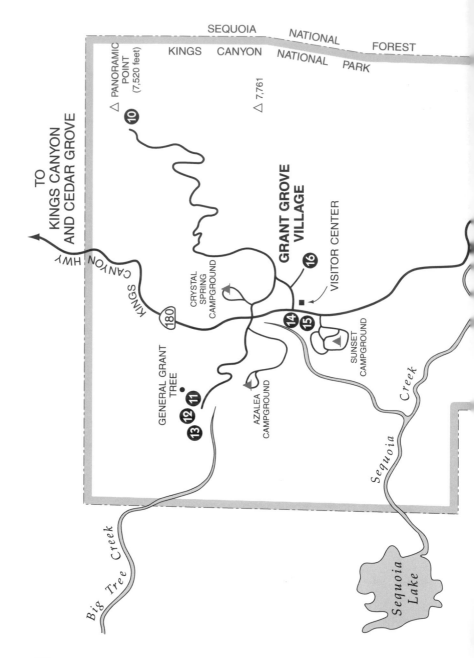

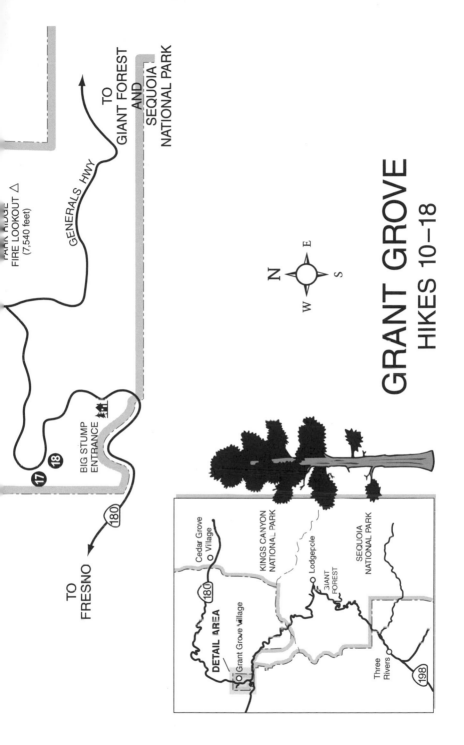

GRANT GROVE
HIKES 10–18

TO
GIANT FOREST
AND
SEQUOIA
NATIONAL PARK

PARK RIDGE
FIRE LOOKOUT △
(7,540 feet)

GENERALS HWY

BIG STUMP
ENTRANCE

17
18

180

TO
FRESNO

N
E
S
W

DETAIL AREA

Cedar Grove
O Village

KINGS CANYON
NATIONAL PARK

O Lodgepole

GIANT
FOREST

SEQUOIA
NATIONAL PARK

180

O Grant Grove Village

Three
Rivers

198

Hike 10
Park Ridge Trail
Panoramic Point to Park Ridge Fire Lookout

Hiking distance: 5 miles round trip
Hiking time: 2.5 hours
Elevation gain: 420 feet
Maps: U.S.G.S. Hume and General Grant Grove
　　　　Sequoia Natural History Association—Grant Grove

Summary of hike: The Park Ridge Trail begins near Panoramic Point, a 7,520-foot overlook with benches and an interpretive display of the peaks and valleys. From the overlook are views of the Middle and South Forks of Kings Canyon, Hume Lake, the Sierra Crest and the Great Western Divide. The trail follows the crest of the ridge to Park Ridge Fire Lookout, an active lookout at 7,540 feet.

Driving directions: From the Grant Grove Visitor Center, drive east through the parking area past the cabins, and bear right up the signed Panoramic Point Road. Continue 2.3 miles to the parking area at the end of the road.

Hiking directions: Head east on the paved trail, climbing for 300 yards to Panoramic Point. The paved trail ends at the overlook, and the single track Park Ridge Trail begins. Follow the ridge south through forest and open areas, with frequent small dips and rises, to a knoll at one mile. There are alternating views of the Monarch Divide and Great Western Divide on the left and the San Joaquin Valley on the right. Descend to a junction with the fire road at 1.5 miles. Bear left on the road for 50 yards, and watch for a signed junction with the Manzanita and Azalea Trail on the right. The sign is set back off the trail. From the sign, take the left fork towards the Park Ridge Fire Lookout. At 2.4 miles the trail rejoins the fire road. Bear to the right for 0.2 miles to the fire lookout. After enjoying the spectacular views, return on the fire road all the way back to Panoramic Point Road. Turn right and head 100 yards back to the parking area.

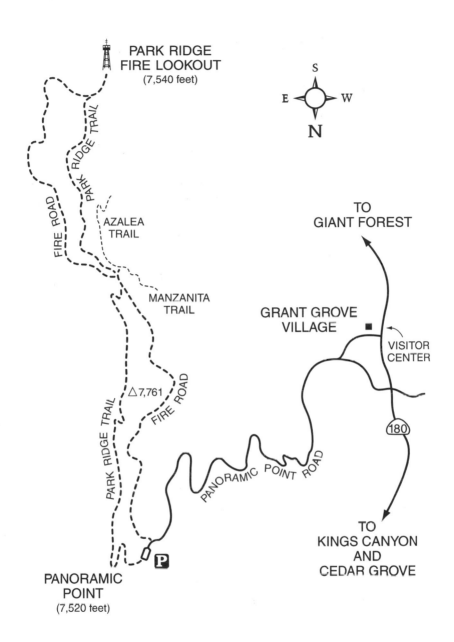

PARK RIDGE TRAIL

Hike 11
General Grant Tree Trail

Hiking distance: 1 mile loop
Hiking time: 30 minutes
Elevation gain: 80 feet
Maps: U.S.G.S. General Grant Grove
Sequoia Natural History Association—Grant Grove

Summary of hike: The General Grant Tree Trail loops through a beautiful grove with a dense concentration of giant sequoias. Interpretive signs identify names, historical events, forest features and information about the various sequoias. The 2,000-year-old General Grant Tree is the third largest living tree in the world, standing at 267 feet with a base diameter of 40 feet. At the north end of the loop is the Gamlin Cabin, built in 1872 from sugar pine trees. The cabin, once home to the Gamlin brothers, was also used as a ranger station, museum and storage facility by the U.S. Cavalry. Part of the trail is wheelchair accessible.

Driving directions: From the Grant Grove Visitor Center, take Highway 180 for 0.2 miles north to the Azalea/Columbine turnoff on the left. Turn left and continue 0.8 miles down the winding road to the Grant Tree parking lot on the right.

Hiking directions: From the trailhead information board, take the right fork past the Robert E. Lee tree to the Fallen Monarch. Take a short detour through the length of the 124–foot hollow giant sequoia, once used to house people and stable horses. The main trail continues to a loop circling the General Grant Tree. Continue up to the Gamlin Pioneer Cabin at the northern tip of the trail. The return route to the left passes the Centennial Stump, California, Oregon and Lincoln trees before returning to the trailhead.

To hike further, continue your walk with Hikes 12 and 13.

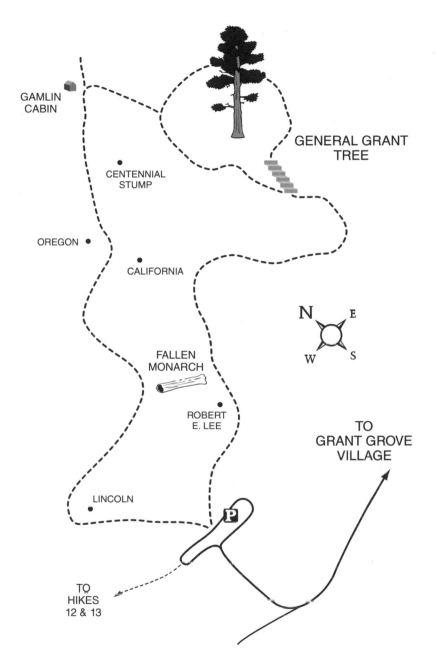

GAMLIN
CABIN

GENERAL GRANT
TREE

CENTENNIAL
STUMP

OREGON

CALIFORNIA

N
E
W
S

FALLEN
MONARCH

ROBERT
E. LEE

TO
GRANT GROVE
VILLAGE

LINCOLN

P

TO
HIKES
12 & 13

GENERAL GRANT TREE

Hike 12
North Grove Loop Trail

Hiking distance: 2 mile loop
Hiking time: 1 hour
Elevation gain: 400 feet
Maps: U.S.G.S. General Grant Grove
      Sequoia Natural History Association—Grant Grove

Summary of hike: The North Grove Loop Trail begins at the Grant Tree parking area and follows an unpaved road through the forest. The trail loops through groves of giant sequoias, white fir, sugar pines and dogwood. At the north end of the loop is an old logging road that was used by wagons in the late 1800s.

Driving directions: From the Grant Grove Visitor Center, take Highway 180 for 0.2 miles north to the Azalea/Columbine turnoff on the left. Turn left and continue 0.8 miles down the winding road to the Grant Tree parking lot. The trailhead is on the left, at the west end of the parking lot reserved for buses and RVs.

Hiking directions: Head west past the trailhead sign and gate on the fire road to a junction 100 yards ahead. The Sunset Trail (Hike 14) continues straight ahead. Take the right fork downhill on the North Grove Loop. The trail descends deep into the forest. At the bottom, curve to the left (west) past Old Millwood Road on the right, an old wagon road once used for logging. Stay on the main trail, heading south and steadily climbing to regain elevation. At 1.5 miles, the trail rejoins the Sunset Trail. Take the left fork uphill and return to the trailhead.

To hike further, continue on the Dead Giant Loop Trail (Hike 13) or the General Grant Tree Trail (Hike 11).

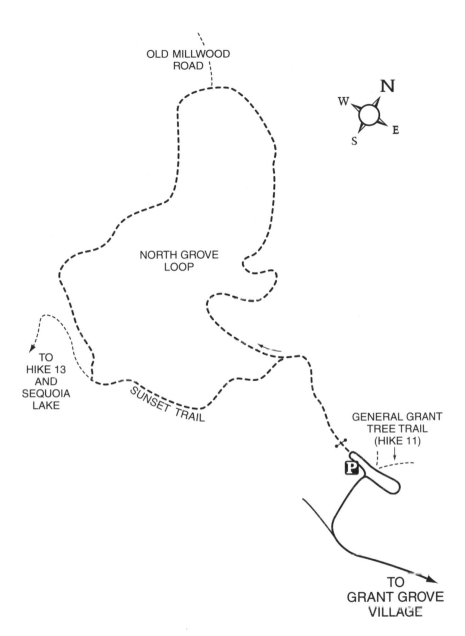

OLD MILLWOOD
ROAD

N
W E
S

NORTH GROVE
LOOP

TO
HIKE 13
AND
SEQUOIA
LAKE

SUNSET TRAIL

GENERAL GRANT
TREE TRAIL
(HIKE 11)

P

TO
GRANT GROVE
VILLAGE

NORTH GROVE
LOOP TRAIL

Hike 13
Dead Giant Loop Trail

Hiking distance: 2.3 miles round trip
Hiking time: 1 hour
Elevation gain: 250 feet
Maps: U.S.G.S. General Grant Grove
Sequoia Natural History Association—Grant Grove

Summary of hike: The Dead Giant Loop Trail heads downhill into a sequoia, fir and pine forest. The trail passes Dead Giant, a massive sequoia axed by loggers. The trail continues to a knoll at the Sequoia Lake Overlook.

Driving directions: From the Grant Grove Visitor Center, take Highway 180 for 0.2 miles north to the Azalea/Columbine turnoff on the left. Turn left and continue 0.8 miles down the winding road to the Grant Tree parking lot. The trailhead is on the left, at the west end of the parking lot reserved for buses and RVs.

Hiking directions: Hike west past the trailhead sign on the closed road. A short distance ahead is a junction with the North Grove Loop Trail (Hike 12). Continue straight ahead on the Sunset Trail towards Sequoia Lake to a second junction with the North Grove Loop Trail. Again, stay on the main trail, passing Lion Meadow on the right, to the signed junction with the Dead Giant Trail at 0.75 miles. Take the footpath on the right, and head north to the Dead Giant. Beyond the Dead Giant, the trail curves left, circling the knoll to a 6,000-foot overlook of Sequoia Lake. Past the overlook, the trail rejoins the Sunset Trail. Take the road left, returning to the trailhead.

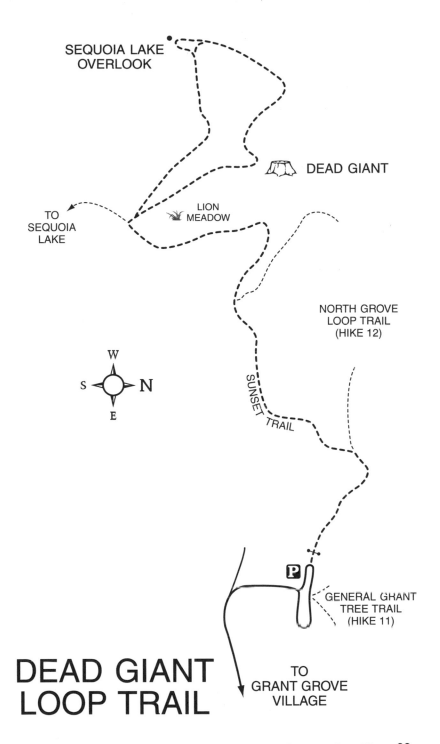

SEQUOIA LAKE
OVERLOOK

DEAD GIANT

TO
SEQUOIA
LAKE

LION
MEADOW

NORTH GROVE
LOOP TRAIL
(HIKE 12)

W

S ● N

E

SUNSET TRAIL

P

GENERAL GRANT
TREE TRAIL
(HIKE 11)

DEAD GIANT
LOOP TRAIL

TO
GRANT GROVE
VILLAGE

Hike 14
Sunset Trail

Hiking distance: 6 mile loop
Hiking time: 3 hours
Elevation gain: 1,200 feet
Maps: U.S.G.S. General Grant Grove
  Sequoia Natural History Association—Grant Grove

Summary of hike: The Sunset Trail is a forested loop hike from Grant Grove Village that crosses wooden bridges, follows a portion of Sequoia Creek and leads to Sequoia Lake. The trail passes Ella Falls, a narrow 40-foot cascade, and pools etched in granite bowls. The area is surrounded by lush azaleas, willows and alders.

Driving directions: This hike begins at the Grant Grove Visitor Center.

Hiking directions: Cross Highway 180, curving left on the path between Sunset Campground and the highway to the campground entrance road. Follow the Sunset Campground road to the south end. The signed trailhead to Ella Falls is on the west side of campsite 179. Take the footpath down switchbacks past large boulders, leading deep into the forested canyon. At one mile, cross a footbridge over a rock-enclosed cascade with pools. Descend to a four-way junction with the South Boundary Trail (Hike 15). Take the middle fork downhill towards Ella Falls and Sequoia Lake. Past the falls, the trail crosses the park boundary to a privately owned YMCA camp and a junction. The left fork leads to Sequoia Lake. Bear right, heading uphill to the north on the Sunset Trail. A short distance ahead is a junction with an old fire road. Take this road, reentering the national park. Pass junctions with the Dead Giant and North Grove Loops to the General Grant Tree parking lot. Pick up the trail again on the east side of the lot. The footpath curves right and crosses the paved road. Head uphill to the Azalea Campground, across the highway from Grant Grove Village.

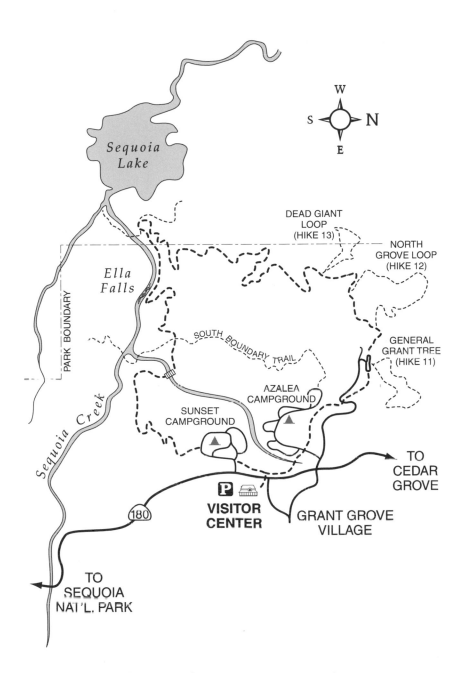

SUNSET TRAIL

Hike 15
South Boundary Trail

Hiking distance: 5 mile loop
Hiking time: 2.5 hours
Elevation gain: 650 feet
Maps: U.S.G.S. General Grant Grove
      Sequoia Natural History Association—Grant Grove

Summary of hike: The South Boundary Trail is a loop hike through the dense forest around the Grant Grove area. The trail passes Viola Falls, a series of small waterfalls with bowl-shaped pools etched into the granite rock. A short detour leads to Ella Falls, a beautiful 40-foot cascade in Sequoia Creek.

Driving directions: This hike begins at the Grant Grove Visitor Center.

Hiking directions: Cross Highway 180 and descend on the paved path to the campground amphitheater. Head north across a meadow into the Azalea Campground. Follow the campground road to the far northwest corner. The signed South Boundary Trail is to the west of campsite 110. Take the trail a short distance downhill and bear left, continuing downhill. At one mile, the Swale Work Center can be seen on the right. Take the signed trail on the left, heading south through the forest. Continue past several cabins to an old, narrow, unpaved road. Bear left on the road to the signed four-way junction with the Sunset Trail (Hike 14). For a great side trip, take the right fork a half mile on the Sunset Trail to Ella Falls. Back at the junction, continue south to Sequoia Creek a quarter mile ahead. Take the side path to the right a hundred yards downstream to Viola Falls. Return to the main trail, and cross Sequoia Creek heading south past giant sequoias and logged stumps. Continue to a junction with the Hitchcock Meadow Trail (Hike 17). Bear left, heading uphill to the east. Cross Sequoia Creek on a wooden bridge, and continue uphill to Highway 180. Cross the highway to the signed Azalea Trail (Hike 16). Take the Azalea Trail left, and cross a log bridge before recrossing to the west side of Highway 180. Head north past the Sunset Campground to the amphitheater, across the road from the visitor center.

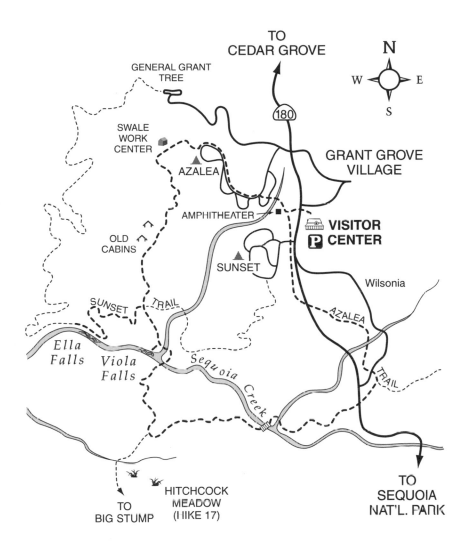

SOUTH BOUNDARY TRAIL

Hike 16
Manzanita and Azalea Loop

Hiking distance: 5 mile loop
Hiking time: 2.5 hours
Elevation gain: 800 feet
Maps: U.S.G.S. General Grant Grove
Sequoia Natural History Association—Grant Grove

Summary of hike: The Manzanita Trail climbs for one mile up the eastern slope of a mountain to Park Ridge. From the ridge, the Azalea Trail follows a fern-lined tributary stream of Sequoia Creek down through the moist, shady forest, returning to Grant Grove Village. The stream banks are lined with ferns and azaleas.

Driving directions: This hike begins at the Grant Grove Visitor Center.

Hiking directions: Walk east through the parking lot and past the camping cabins to the first road on the right marked "Residential Area Only." Head up the road 0.4 miles to the signed Manzanita Trail on the right, before the water tank. Take the trail east, gaining elevation up the mountainside. Continue past the Crystal Spring Trail and the Round Meadow Trail, both coming in from the left. At 1.5 miles is a five-way junction with the Park Ridge Trail and fire road, which lead to Panoramic Point and the Park Ridge Fire Lookout (Hike 10). Take the signed Azalea Trail to the right, returning downhill through the dense forest alongside a tributary stream of Sequoia Creek. Cross two wooden bridges over the creek. After the second crossing, the trail passes the town of Wilsonia. At 3.5 miles is a signed junction with the South Boundary Trail (Hike 15) at Highway 180. Take the right fork on the Azalea Trail (without crossing the highway) and recross the creek. Continue past some cabins and across a log bridge over a stream. Cross Highway 180 and head north, parallel to the highway into Sunset Campground, and return to Grant Grove Village.

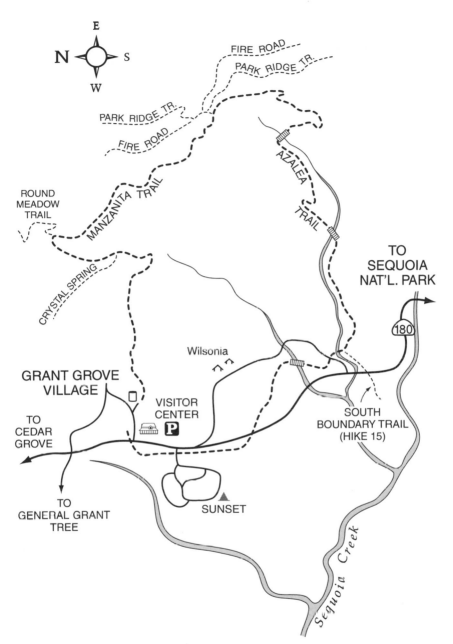

MANZANITA AND AZALEA LOOP

Hike 17
Hitchcock Meadow Trail to Viola Falls

Hiking distance: 3.5 miles round trip
Hiking time: 1.5 hours
Elevation gain: 350 feet
Maps: U.S.G.S. General Grant Grove
       Sequoia Natural History Association—Grant Grove

Summary of hike: Hitchcock Meadow is a small, scenic meadow surrounded by enormous giant sequoia stumps, heavily logged between 1883 and 1889. This hike crosses Hitchcock Meadow to Sequoia Creek and Viola Falls. The falls is a series of stair-stepping waterfalls cascading into sculpted pools in the granite rock.

Driving directions: From the Grant Grove Visitor Center, drive 2.4 miles south on Highway 180, bearing left towards Fresno, to the Big Stump Picnic Area and parking lot on the right. The parking lot is 0.6 miles north of the Big Stump entrance.

Hiking directions: Head west on the signed Hitchcock Meadow Trail, immediately entering the lush forest. Descend gradually to the valley floor, carpeted with ferns and surrounded by giant sequoias and logged sequoia stumps. At 1.2 miles is a junction with the South Boundary Trail (Hike 15). Take the left fork north. Cross Sequoia Creek on a bridge and cross a tributary stream on a culvert. Just beyond the second crossing is a junction. Bear left, following Sequoia Creek downstream 0.1 mile to the granite pools at Viola Falls. After enjoying the falls, return by retracing your steps.

To extend your hike, continue on the Big Stump Loop, Hike 18.

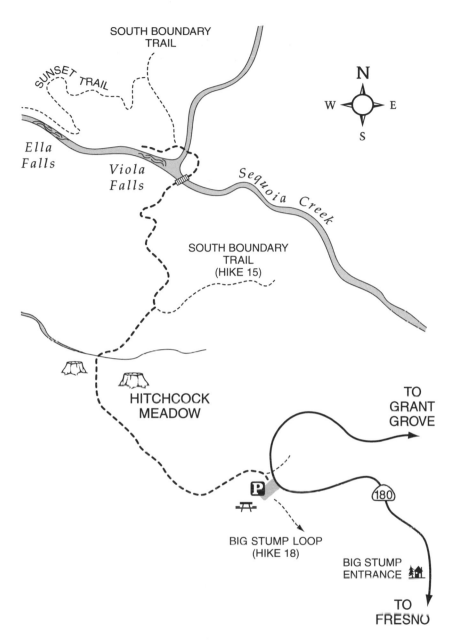

HITCHCOCK MEADOW
TRAIL

Hike 18
Big Stump Loop

Hiking distance: 1.5 miles round trip
Hiking time: 1 hour
Elevation gain: 200 feet
Maps: U.S.G.S. General Grant Grove
Sequoia Natural History Association—Grant Grove

Summary of hike: The Big Stump Basin was logged for timber in the 1880s. These stumps are massive. The hike loops through the gutted grove past a continuous series of stunning stumps, standing giant sequoias and the lumber mill site with piles of 100-year-old sawdust.

Driving directions: From the Grant Grove Visitor Center, drive 2.4 miles south on Highway 180, bearing left towards Fresno, to the Big Stump Picnic Area and parking lot on the right. The parking lot is 0.6 miles north of the Big Stump Entrance Station.

Hiking directions: The trail begins by the restrooms. Head downhill into the forested basin past Resurrection Tree, a lightening-struck topless giant sequoia that still flourishes. At 0.2 miles, take the right fork at a junction towards Shattered Giant, a felled sequoia that split into pieces upon impact. Continue east to another junction. Take the left fork for a short detour to the 1883 Smith Comstock Mill Site, a meadow with large fresh-looking piles of sequoia sawdust collected between 1883 and 1889. Past the mill site is Burnt Monarch, an enormous dead-standing sequoia. Retrace your steps past the mill site and take the Feather Bed Trail to the left, returning to the main loop. Bear left and cross a bridge to the Mark Twain Stump, cut in 1891. A stairway leads to the top. Ahead the trail crosses Highway 180 near the park entrance. After crossing, head north past more stumps to a junction. Take the hundred yard detour to the right up to Sawed Tree, a healthy, partially logged but not toppled sequoia. Back on the main trail, cross under Highway 180 through a culvert to a junction. Take the left fork, completing the loop.

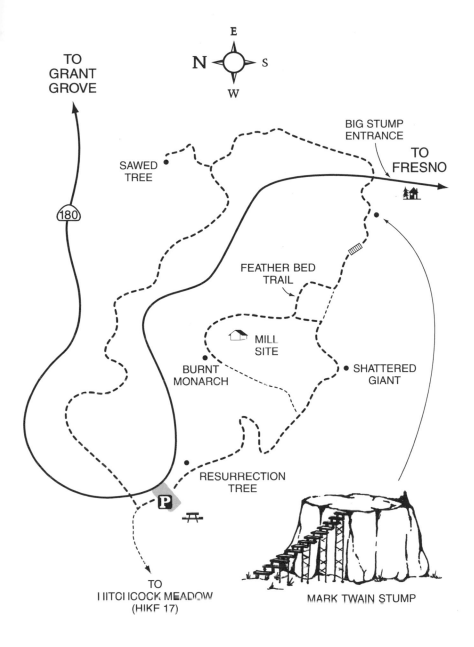

N E S W

TO GRANT GROVE

TO FRESNO

BIG STUMP ENTRANCE

SAWED TREE

180

FEATHER BED TRAIL

MILL SITE

BURNT MONARCH

SHATTERED GIANT

P

RESURRECTION TREE

TO HITCHCOCK MEADOW
(HIKE 17)

MARK TWAIN STUMP

BIG STUMP LOOP

Hike 19
Sugarbowl and Redwood Creek Loop

Hiking distance: 6.5 mile loop
Hiking time: 3 hours
Elevation gain: 1,200 feet
Maps: U.S.G.S. General Grant Grove

map
next page

Summary of hike: Sugarbowl Grove is a dense grove of giant sequoias that will dwarf and humble anyone. The trail follows the forested ridge of Redwood Mountain on the west edge of Redwood Canyon. From the awesome solitude of Sugarbowl Grove, the trail descends to the canyon floor and returns up the canyon parallel to Redwood Creek.

Driving directions: From the Grant Grove Visitor Center, drive 5 miles southbound on Highway 180, bearing left onto the Generals Highway, to a four-way junction with the Hume Lake Road on the left. Turn right on the unpaved road, and head 1.8 miles down the narrow, winding road to a road split. Bear left and park in the Redwood Saddle Trailhead parking lot.

From Stony Creek Village, drive 7.9 miles northwest on the Generals Highway to the four-way junction and turn left.

Hiking directions: Take the signed Sugarbowl Trail uphill to the right to the ridge at 0.4 miles. Giant sequoias are everywhere. At 1.5 miles, switchbacks lead to a great overlook of Big Baldy (Hike 22). Down in Redwood Canyon, the tree tops of the giant sequoias stand out high above the cedars. Continue to the summit near a rock outcropping and another overlook at 2 miles. Descend into a dense grove of young giant sequoias called the Sugarbowl. This is among the best sequoia groves you will ever see. Wind through the grove to an old wooden mileage sign. From the sign, steeply descend to the east, zigzagging into Redwood Canyon. At 4.5 miles is a junction at the canyon floor by Redwood Creek. Bear left up the canyon past more sequoias, parallel to the creek. At the top of the canyon is a junction with the Hart Tree Trail (Hike 20). Head left to the parking area.

Hike 20
Hart Tree and Redwood Creek Loop

Hiking distance: 6.5 mile loop
Hiking time: 3.5 hours
Elevation gain: 900 feet
Maps: U.S.G.S. General Grant Grove

map
next page

Summary of hike: Redwood Canyon is home to the largest concentration of giant sequoias in the world. The trail loops through the solitude of this lush canyon past hundreds of giant sequoias. Hike through the length of Tunnel Tree and visit a hollowed out sequoia with rock chimneys once used as a cabin. The return along the canyon floor parallels Redwood Creek.

Driving directions: Follow the driving directions for Hike 19.

Hiking directions: Take the signed Redwood Canyon Trail to the left, beginning on the Hart Tree Trail. Pass an abundance of giant sequoias to a junction at 0.3 miles. The hike returns on the right fork. Begin on the Hart Tree Trail to the left. Continue downhill, crossing fern-lined Redwood Creek and a small stream. On the east side of the stream is the log cabin, a downed, hollow giant sequoia used in the late 1800s as a home. Climb along the eastern edge of Redwood Canyon for the next mile. At 2 miles, cross Buena Vista Creek to a boulder garden overlooking the canyon. Buena Vista Peak (Hike 21) is visible to the east and Big Baldy (Hike 22) can be seen in the southeast. At 2.8 miles, hike through the length of Tunnel Tree, a hollowed out giant sequoia. Cross the East Fork of Redwood Creek to a signed spur trail on the left up to Hart Tree. Continue on the main trail past a small waterfall. At 4 miles, take the signed right fork to Fallen Goliath, another downed sequoia that one can walk through. Loop back and rejoin the main trail, crossing Redwood Creek at 4.5 miles to a junction. Bear right on the Redwood Creek Trail up the canyon, parallel to Redwood Creek. Pass the Sugarbowl Trail junction on the left (Hike 19), and continue uphill, completing the loop near the top. Bear left, returning to the trailhead.

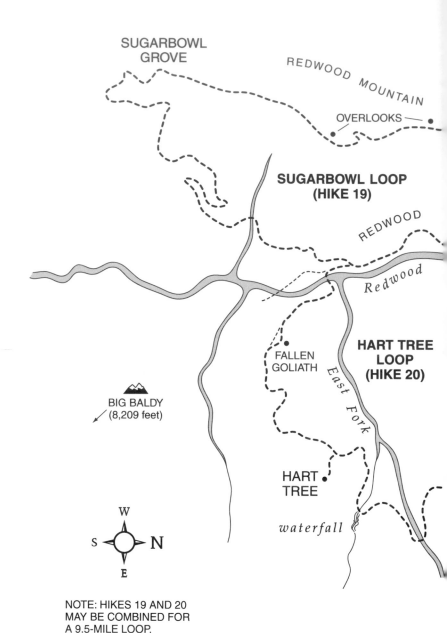

SUGARBOWL
GROVE

REDWOOD MOUNTAIN

OVERLOOKS

SUGARBOWL LOOP
(HIKE 19)

REDWOOD

Redwood

FALLEN
GOLIATH

HART TREE
LOOP
(HIKE 20)

East Fork

BIG BALDY
(8,209 feet)

HART
TREE

waterfall

W
S N
E

NOTE: HIKES 19 AND 20
MAY BE COMBINED FOR
A 9.5-MILE LOOP.

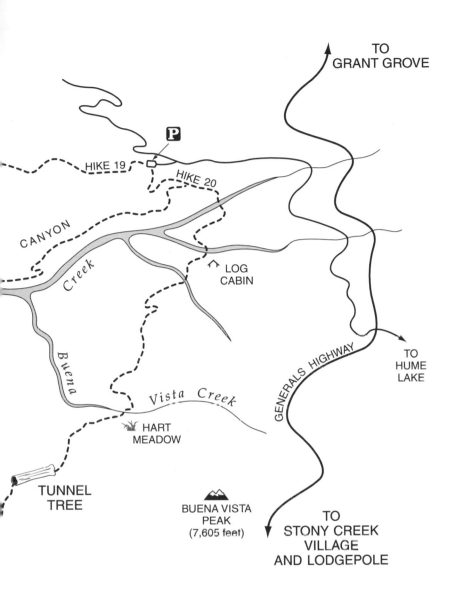

REDWOOD CANYON

SUGARBOWL TRAIL
AND
HART TREE TRAIL

Hike 21
Buena Vista Peak

Hiking distance: 2 miles round trip
Hiking time: 1 hour
Elevation gain: 450 feet
Maps: U.S.G.S. General Grant Grove
Sequoia Natural History Association—Grant Grove

Summary of hike: Buena Vista Peak is a large, rounded granite dome at 7,605 feet. Several gnarled, twisted Jeffrey pines grow on the dome. Buena Vista, meaning "good view" in Spanish, has great views in every direction. Below the peak is Hart Meadow (Hike 20). To the west, across Redwood Canyon, is Redwood Mountain and the Sierra foothills. The snow-capped peaks of the Monarch Divide can be seen in the north. To the east is Kings Canyon and the peaks of the Great Western Divide.

Driving directions: From the Grant Grove Visitor Center, drive 6.1 miles south on Highway 180, bearing left onto Generals Highway at the road split, to the Buena Vista Trailhead parking area on the right. It is located 200 yards beyond the Kings Canyon Overlook.

From Stony Creek Village, drive 6.8 miles northwest on the Generals Highway to the parking area on the left.

Hiking directions: Head northwest past the trailhead sign. Continue uphill past large granite slabs and boulders through a forest of manzanita, cedar, fir and pine. At a quarter mile, the sculpted grey dome of Buena Vista Peak comes into view straight ahead. The trail contours around the left side of the dome to an overlook on the south. From the overlook, head up the ridge to the large weathered rocks on the dome. From the summit, Big Baldy (Hike 22) can be seen to the south. After enjoying the views, return along the same path.

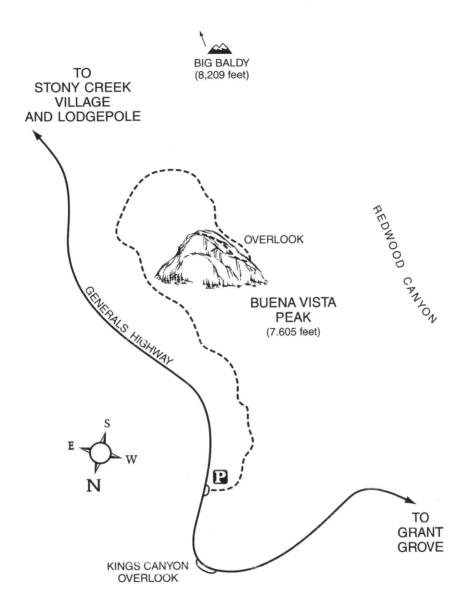

BIG BALDY
(8,209 feet)

TO
STONY CREEK
VILLAGE
AND LODGEPOLE

OVERLOOK

REDWOOD CANYON

GENERALS HIGHWAY

BUENA VISTA
PEAK
(7.605 feet)

S
E · W
N

P

TO
GRANT
GROVE

KINGS CANYON
OVERLOOK

BUENA VISTA PEAK

Hike 22
Big Baldy

Hiking distance: 5 miles round trip
Hiking time: 2.5 hours
Elevation gain: 600 feet
Maps: U.S.G.S. General Grant Grove
　　　　Sequoia Natural History Association—Grant Grove

Summary of hike: Big Baldy is a bare, rocky knob with great panoramas in every direction. A forested path to the 8,209-foot summit follows a ridge with several overlooks along the east wall of Redwood Canyon. Redwood Mountain, Sugarbowl Grove and the foothills can be seen in the distance.

Driving directions: From the Grant Grove Visitor Center, drive 8.1 miles south on Highway 180, bearing left onto Generals Highway at the road split, to the Big Baldy trailhead parking pull-outs along the right side of the road. The pullouts are on a bend in the road by the wooden trailhead sign.

From Stony Creek Village, drive 4.8 miles northwest on the Generals Highway to the pullouts on the left.

Hiking directions: Head south away from the highway, immediately entering a dense fir forest. Disregard the faint trails on the left, and stay on the well-defined main trail. Continue uphill to an overlook of Redwood Canyon at 0.5 miles. Across the canyon, on the ridge of Redwood Mountain, is Sugarbowl Grove. The grove is a distinctive dense cluster of giant sequoias (Hike 19). Reenter the forest before reaching a second overlook at one mile, where there is a full view of Big Baldy to the south. The trail follows the ridge overlooking Redwood Canyon towards the final ascent of Big Baldy. The rock-lined trail winds up to an awesome summit. At the top, a 1950 survey pin is embedded in the rock. You may continue a half mile beyond the summit to a knoll with more outstanding views. To return, take the same path back.

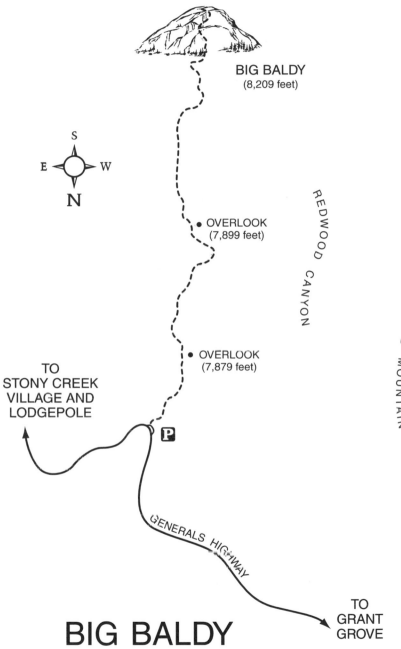

BIG BALDY
(8,209 feet)

S
E   W
N

OVERLOOK
(7,899 feet)

REDWOOD CANYON

REDWOOD MOUNTAIN

OVERLOOK
(7,879 feet)

TO
STONY CREEK
VILLAGE AND
LODGEPOLE

P

GENERALS HIGHWAY

TO
GRANT
GROVE

BIG BALDY

Hike 23
Lost Grove Trail

Hiking distance: 5.2 miles round trip
Hiking time: 2.5 hours
Elevation gain: 250 feet
Maps: U.S.G.S. Muir Grove

Summary of hike: Lost Grove, covering 54 acres, is among the densest concentrations of giant sequoias in Sequoia National Park. There are more than 400 giant sequoias. The Lost Grove Trail begins in Dorst Campground and parallels the Dorst Creek drainage to the grove. The Generals Highway bisects Lost Grove. A short, handicapped accessible trail explores a hillside grove on the northeast side of the road.

Driving directions: From Stony Creek Village, drive 5 miles southeast on the Generals Highway to Dorst Campground on the right (west). Turn right and drive into the campground to the signed "Group Campground" on the right. Turn right and quickly turn right again at the first road. Park in the spaces on the left by campsite B. (The campground is 18 miles southeast of Grant Grove Village.)

From Lodgepole, drive 8.1 miles northwest on the Generals Highway to Dorst Campground and turn left.

Hiking directions: Cross the campground road to Cabin Creek at the signed trailhead on the left. Bear left and head north along Cabin Creek. At a half mile, descend to Dorst Creek. Rock hop across the creek and pick up the trail to the right. A short distance ahead is a signed junction. The right fork continues on the Cabin Creek Trail. Take the left fork, traversing the hillside high above Dorst Creek. Descend into the canyon in a white fir forest, following the drainage through lush ferns and willows to a signed junction at 2.1 miles. The left fork leads 0.4 miles to the park boundary at Generals Highway. Take the right fork into the lower end of Lost Grove as a few giant sequoias begin to appear. Cross a small stream into the heart of Lost

Grove, surrounded by clusters of large sequoias. Switchbacks lead steeply uphill through the grove, reaching the Generals Highway at 2.5 miles. Across the highway, the trail follows a paved path on the hillside. Return along the same path.

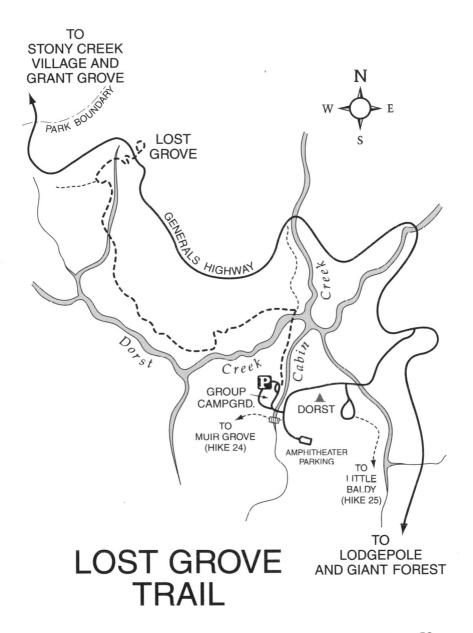

LOST GROVE TRAIL

Hike 24
Muir Grove Trail

Hiking distance: 4 miles round trip
Hiking time: 2 hours
Elevation gain: 250 feet
Maps: U.S.G.S. Muir Grove

Summary of hike: Muir Grove is an undisturbed grove of giant sequoias in a pristine forest away from the crowds. The trailhead is in Dorst Campground. The path to the secluded grove follows a beautiful fern-filled forest of red fir, white fir, cedar and sugar pine trees. There are several stream crossings and a vista overlook.

Driving directions: From Stony Creek Village, drive 5 miles southeast on Generals Highway to Dorst Campground on the right (west). Turn right and drive 0.6 miles into the campground to the signed trail on the right, just past the group campground. Park 50 yards past the trailhead in the amphitheater parking lot. (The campground is 18 miles southeast of Grant Grove Village.)

From Lodgepole, drive 8.1 miles northwest on the Generals Highway to Dorst Campground and turn left.

Hiking directions: Walk back 50 yards to the signed trailhead, and cross the log bridge over Cabin Creek. Descend into the dense forest to a trail split at 0.1 mile. Bear left and traverse the hillside above the Dorst Creek drainage. At a half mile, cross a stream over granite rock, and continue through the lush forest. Begin a steady but moderate climb to the high point of the trail at an overlook on the right atop a bare granite dome. Looking across the canyon to the west, the sequoias of Muir Grove can be spotted along the ridge. Return to the trail and descend, crossing a tributary of Dorst Creek at 1.5 miles. Curve sharply to the right and head north, reaching a remote grove of giant sequoias on the ridge. This is Muir Grove. Various paths meander through the grove. To return, retrace your steps.

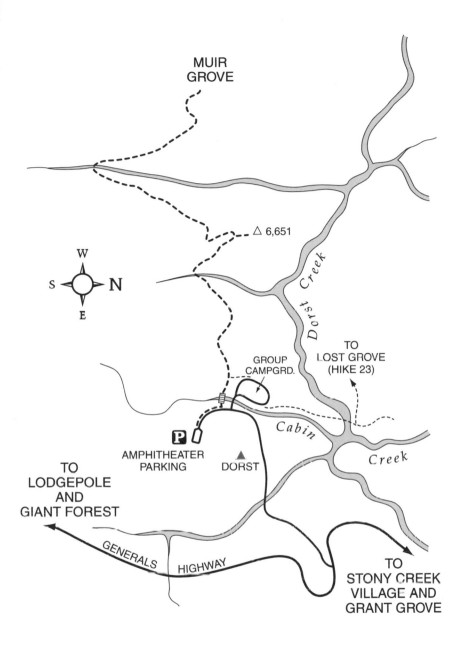

MUIR GROVE

△ 6,651

Dorst Creek

W
S ✦ N
E

TO
LOST GROVE
(HIKE 23)

GROUP
CAMPGRD.

Cabin

P
AMPHITHEATER
PARKING   ▲ DORST

Creek

TO
LODGEPOLE
AND
GIANT FOREST

GENERALS HIGHWAY

TO
STONY CREEK
VILLAGE AND
GRANT GROVE

MUIR GROVE
TRAIL

Hike 25
Little Baldy Trail

Hiking distance: 3.4 miles round trip
Hiking time: 2 hours
Elevation gain: 700 feet
Maps: U.S.G.S. Giant Forest

Summary of hike: Little Baldy, once used as a fire lookout, is a smooth, rounded granite dome with a commanding 360-degree panoramic view. The summit is considered by many to offer the best views of any hike in Sequoia National Park. To the east and southeast are Castle Rocks, Sawtooth Peak, Silliman Crest, Mineral King and the Great Western Divide. To the northwest is Chimney Rock and Big Baldy. To the south are the many canyons and ridges along the Kaweah River Canyon.

Driving directions: From Lodgepole, drive 6.6 miles northwest on the Generals Highway to the Little Baldy Saddle and the signed trailhead parking pullout on the right (east). From Dorst Campground, drive 1.5 miles south on Generals Highway to the signed trailhead parking pullout on the left.

Hiking directions: Walk up the steps, entering the old growth red fir and Jeffrey pine forest. Long easy switchbacks lead up the mountain, steadily gaining elevation. At 1.3 miles the path levels out on the mountain ridgetop by a knoll on the right. To the northwest is the jagged Chimney Rock formation with the rounded bare rock of Big Baldy prominently behind it (Hike 22). Continue south, crossing the level ridge through oaks and manzanita bushes, to the base of Little Baldy. A short climb with natural rock steps leads to the broad rocky summit. A geological survey pin is embedded in the granite peak. After marveling at the magnificent views, return along the same trail.

Little Baldy may also be accessed from the Dorst Campground by taking the Little Baldy Saddle Trail. Dorst Campground is 1.5 miles from Little Baldy Saddle.

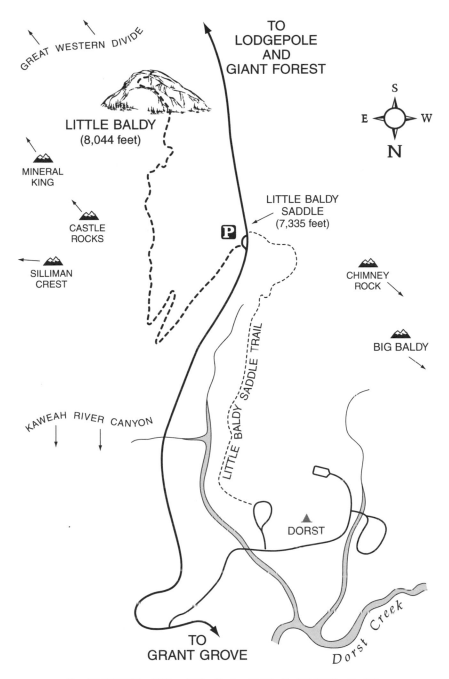

GREAT WESTERN DIVIDE

TO
LODGEPOLE
AND
GIANT FOREST

LITTLE BALDY
(8,044 feet)

S

E — W

N

MINERAL
KING

CASTLE
ROCKS

LITTLE BALDY
SADDLE
(7,335 feet)

P

SILLIMAN
CREST

CHIMNEY
ROCK

BIG BALDY

LITTLE BALDY SADDLE TRAIL

KAWEAH RIVER CANYON

DORST

TO
GRANT GROVE

Dorst Creek

LITTLE BALDY TRAIL

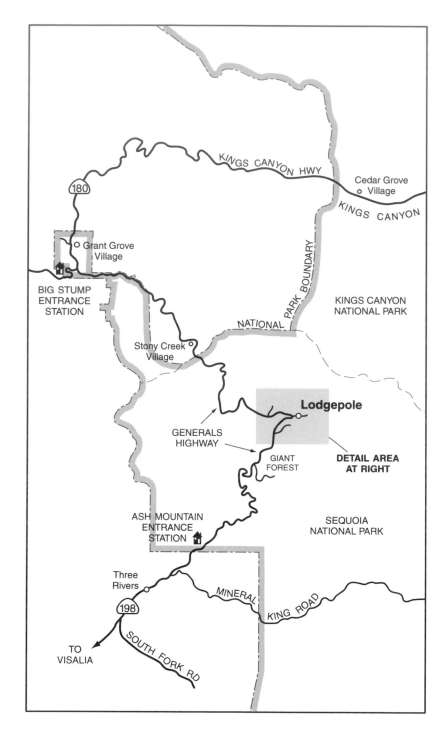

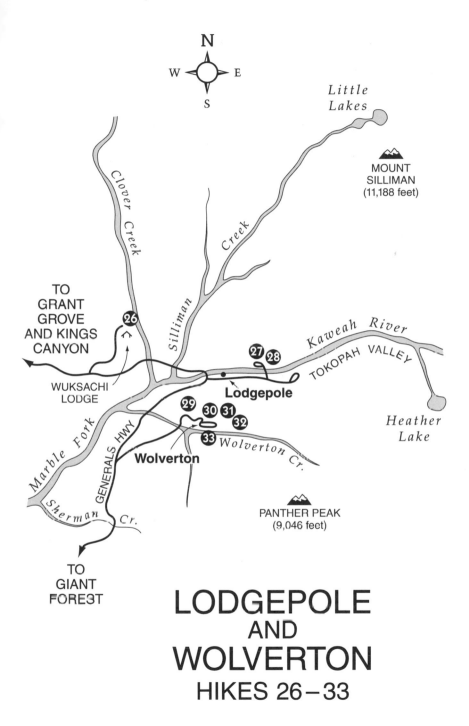

LODGEPOLE
AND
WOLVERTON
HIKES 26–33

Hike 26
Wuksachi Trail to Twin Lakes Trail

Hiking distance: 3 miles round trip
Hiking time: 1.5 hours
Elevation gain: 300 feet
Maps: U.S.G.S. Giant Forest and Lodgepole

Summary of hike: For a pastoral forest hike away from the crowds, the Wuksachi Trail is a little gem. The trail connects Wuksachi Village with Lodgepole. The route crosses two beautiful new bridges over Clover Creek and Silliman Creek. This newer path, not shown on the U.S.G.S. maps, has a panoramic overlook of the valley below.

Driving directions: From Lodgepole, drive 1.6 miles west to the signed Wuksachi Village turnoff and turn right. Continue one mile, passing the village center, to the parking lot at the end of the road. The signed trail is on the north side of the lot.

Hiking directions: Head east on the wide path, entering a pine and fir forest. Four switchbacks lead down the hillside to the Clover Creek drainage. Cross the large wooden bridge over Clover Creek in a rocky gorge by a series of pools. Switchbacks wind up the forested hillside away from the creek. At 0.8 miles, the path reaches a clearing with a view across Lodgepole to the Wolverton ridge. Curve northeast, following the contour of the hillside to the rocky gorge at Silliman Creek. Parallel the creek upstream for a short distance to an L-shaped log bridge spanning the creek. Cross to the east side of Silliman Creek, and follow a small tributary stream to a T-junction with the Twin Lakes Trail. This is the turnaround spot.

To hike further, the right fork descends 1.6 miles to Lodgepole at the Twin Lakes trailhead (Hike 27). The left fork leads one mile to Cahoon Meadow and continues to Twin Lakes.

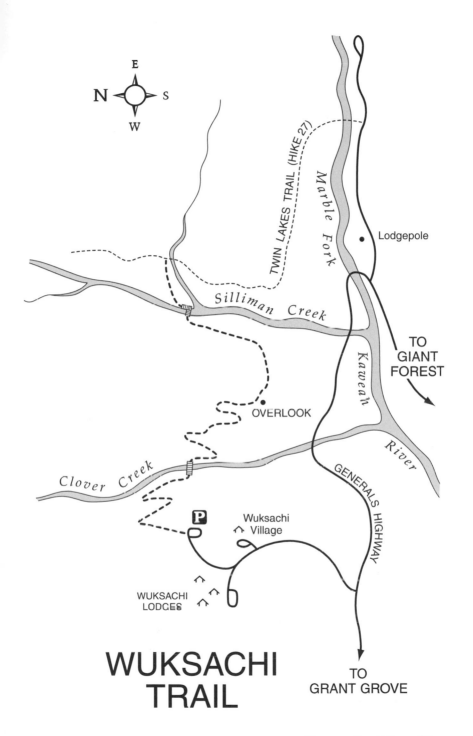

E N S W

TWIN LAKES TRAIL (HIKE 27)

Marble Fork

Lodgepole

Silliman Creek

Kaweah

TO
GIANT
FOREST

OVERLOOK

River

Clover Creek

GENERALS HIGHWAY

P

Wuksachi
Village

WUKSACHI
LODGES

WUKSACHI
TRAIL

TO
GRANT GROVE

Hike 27
Twin Lakes Trail to Cahoon Meadow

Hiking distance: 5.4 miles round trip
Hiking time: 3 hours
Elevation gain: 1,000 feet
Maps: U.S.G.S. Lodgepole and Mount Silliman
Sequoia Natural History Assc.—Lodgepole/Wolverton

Summary of hike: Cahoon Meadow is a lush, grassy meadow marbled with serpentine streams. The Twin Lakes Trail is not heavily used, making Cahoon Meadow a perfect destination for a scenic, high country hike away from the crowds.

Driving directions: From the Lodgepole turnoff on the Generals Highway, drive 0.6 miles east, passing the visitor center, into the Lodgepole Campground. Use the parking spaces on the left before reaching the bridge over the Marble Fork of the Kaweah River.

Hiking directions: Follow the gated road 50 yards along the Marble Fork of the Kaweah River. Cross the bridge on the left over the river. Fifty yards ahead is the signed Twin Lakes Trail on the right. Take the rock-lined path around Lodgepole Campground. Begin the ascent, traversing the south-facing hillside to the west. The trail levels out, curves north and enters a shady red fir and lodgepole pine forest at one mile. Cross a tributary stream of Silliman Creek and a signed junction by Willow Meadow at 1.6 miles. The Wuksachi Trail (Hike 26) bears left. Continue straight ahead, staying on the Twin Lakes Trail. At the north end of the plateau, switchbacks lead uphill and cross Silliman Creek in a rocky gorge by pools and waterfalls. Curve around the west side of the drainage, reaching the south edge of Cahoon Meadow at 2.5 miles. The trail follows the east edge of the meadow. Several side paths bear left into the open meadow. This is our turnaround spot. Return along the same trail.

To hike further, the trail continues past Cahoon Gap to Clover Creek at 5 miles and Twin Lakes at 6.8 miles.

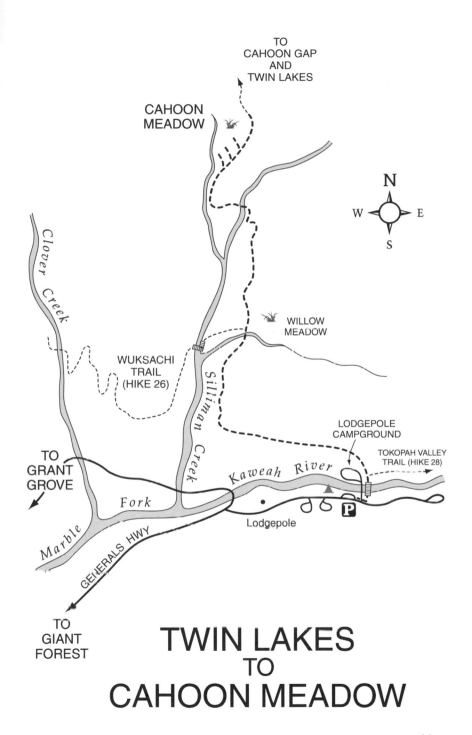

TO
CAHOON GAP
AND
TWIN LAKES

CAHOON
MEADOW

N

W · E

S

Clover Creek

WILLOW
MEADOW

WUKSACHI
TRAIL
(HIKE 26)

Silliman Creek

LODGEPOLE
CAMPGROUND

TO
GRANT
GROVE

Kaweah River

TOKOPAH VALLEY
TRAIL (HIKE 28)

Fork

Marble

P

Lodgepole

GENERALS HWY

TO
GIANT
FOREST

TWIN LAKES
TO
CAHOON MEADOW

Hike 28
Tokopah Valley Trail to Tokopah Falls

Hiking distance: 3.6 miles round trip
Hiking time: 2 hours
Elevation gain: 500 feet
Maps: U.S.G.S. Lodgepole
Sequoia Natural History Assc.—Lodgepole/Wolverton

Summary of hike: Tokopah Falls in the Marble Fork of the Kaweah River is a massive cascade tumbling off the steep granite cliffs at the headwall of a gorgeous valley. This hike follows the river up the glacially carved U-shaped Tokopah Valley through a cedar, pine and fir forest. The trail ends at the base of the falls, surrounded by towering peaks and 1,000-foot sheer rock walls.

Driving directions: From the Lodgepole turnoff on the Generals Highway, drive 0.6 miles east, passing the visitor center, into the Lodgepole Campground. Use the parking spaces on the left before reaching the bridge over the Marble Fork of the Kaweah River.

Hiking directions: Walk up the road and cross Log Bridge, the wooden bridge on the left over the Marble Fork of the Kaweah River. The signed Tokopah Valley Trail bears right, following the north shore of the river upstream. Various side paths lead down to the river. Take the wide, rocky trail past pools etched in the smooth, bowl-shaped rocks. The trail follows a moderate grade most of the way. At 1.3 miles, cross a wooden footbridge over an unnamed creek and another bridge over Horse Creek. The path winds through massive granite boulders to a cirque at the head of the valley. Tokopah Falls cascades off the cliffs. The trail ends at the base of the cirque a short distance from the waterfall. Return on the same trail.

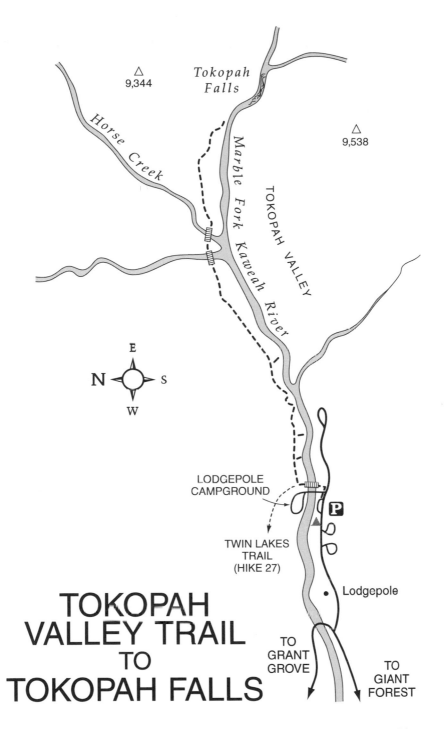

9,344

Tokopah Falls

9,538

Horse Creek

Marble Fork Kaweah River

TOKOPAH VALLEY

E
N ⊕ S
W

LODGEPOLE
CAMPGROUND

P

TWIN LAKES
TRAIL
(HIKE 27)

Lodgepole

TOKOPAH
VALLEY TRAIL
TO
TOKOPAH FALLS

TO
GRANT
GROVE

TO
GIANT
FOREST

Hike 29
Wolverton—Lodgepole Connector Trail

Hiking distance: 3.2 miles round trip
Hiking time: 1.5 hours
Elevation gain: 500 feet
Maps: U.S.G.S. Lodgepole
 Sequoia Natural History Assc.—Lodgepole/Wolverton

Summary of hike: This forested hike begins on the mountain ridge at Wolverton and gradually descends to the Lodgepole Campground near Tokopah Valley. Part of the hike follows the original road connecting Lodgepole and Wolverton before the Generals Highway was built in the 1920s.

Driving directions: The signed Wolverton turnoff is on the Generals Highway 1.6 miles southwest of Lodgepole and 2.5 miles north of Giant Forest Village. Drive 1.4 miles northeast on the Wolverton Road into the large Wolverton parking lot. Turn left and park in the upper north end of the lot by the concrete steps at the signed trailhead.

Hiking directions: Take the signed Lakes Trail up the steps, immediately entering the dense forest. Head uphill 0.1 mile to a signed junction on the mountain ridge overlooking Lodgepole and Tokopah Valley. The Lakes Trail (Hike 30) goes to the right. Bear left towards Lodgepole, and descend on the footpath traversing the hillside to the west. At 0.6 miles, the trail reaches a T-junction at Wolverton Creek. Along the creek are beautiful carved rock formations, pools, cascades and small waterfalls. The left fork leads to the Wolverton corrals. Go to the right, following the old road northeast towards Lodgepole. Wind through the forest down the gentle grade, reaching the Lodgepole Campground east of the visitor center. To return, retrace your steps.

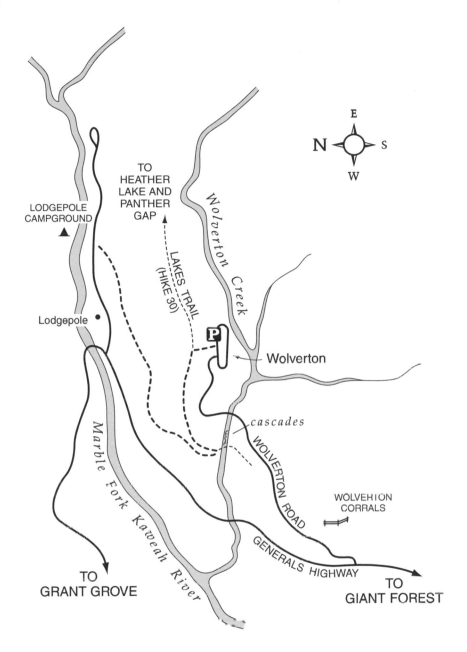

WOLVERTON–LODGEPOLE CONNECTOR TRAIL

Hike 30
Lakes Trail along Wolverton Creek

Hiking distance: 3.6 miles round trip
Hiking time: 2 hours
Elevation gain: 700 feet
Maps: U.S.G.S. Lodgepole
      Sequoia Natural History Assc.—Lodgepole/Wolverton

Summary of hike: The Lakes Trail begins in Wolverton and leads through dense forests to Heather Lake, Emerald Lake and Pear Lake. This hike follows the first portion of the Lakes Trail along Wolverton ridge. The trail parallels Wolverton Creek and has incredible views into Lodgepole and the Tokopah Valley.

Driving directions: The signed Wolverton turnoff is on the Generals Highway 1.6 miles southwest of Lodgepole and 2.5 miles north of Giant Forest Village. Drive 1.4 miles northeast on the Wolverton Road into the large Wolverton parking lot. Turn left and park in the upper north end of the lot by the concrete steps at the signed trailhead.

Hiking directions: Walk up the steps past the trailhead sign, and head north 100 yards to a T-junction on the ridge above Lodgepole. The left fork descends to Lodgepole (Hike 29). Take the right fork uphill along the ridge to the east that overlooks Tokopah Valley. At 0.8 miles, the path levels out by Wolverton Creek and a grassy meadow on the right. Curve southeast, following the creek upstream. Traverse the hillside, heading uphill above Wolverton Creek, and cross a feeder stream at 1.7 miles. Two hundred yards ahead is a signed junction to Heather Lake and Panther Gap. This is the turnaround point.

To hike further, the Lakes Trail continues to the left (Hike 31), reaching Heather Lake 2.3 miles ahead. The Alta Trail to the right (Hike 32) leads past Panther Gap to Mehrten Meadow 2.3 miles ahead.

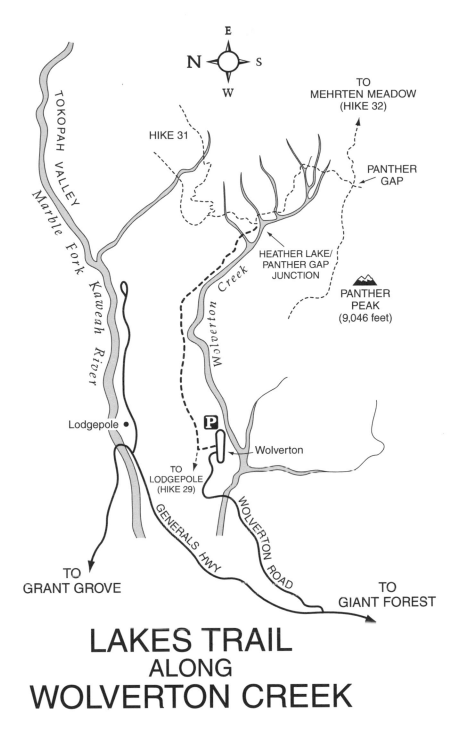

LAKES TRAIL
ALONG
WOLVERTON CREEK

Hike 31
Heather Lake

Hiking distance: 8.2 miles round trip
Hiking time: 4 hours
Elevation gain: 1,900 feet
Maps: U.S.G.S. Lodgepole
         Sequoia Natural History Assc.—Lodgepole/Wolverton

Summary of hike: Heather Lake sits in a picturesque, glacially carved alpine cirque tucked against jagged granite cliffs. This hike begins on the Lakes Trail and connects with the Watchtower and Hump Trails, forming a loop. The hike includes The Watchtower, a 1,600-foot granite promontory extending off the south wall of Tokopah Valley, and the Hump, a 9,500-foot saddle to an overlook of Silliman Crest and the dramatic cliffs at the head of Tokopah Valley.

Driving directions: Follow the driving directions for Hike 30 to the Wolverton parking lot.

Hiking directions: Follow the hiking directions for the Lakes Trail along Wolverton Creek—Hike 30—to the Heather Lake/Panther Gap junction at 1.8 miles. Take the left fork, staying on the Lakes Trail uphill to another junction at 2.1 miles. Both trails lead to Heather Lake. Begin the loop on the left fork—the Watchtower Trail—a more gradual and scenic ascent. Follow the rocky ledge on a narrow vertical wall high above Tokopah Valley. The trail passes The Watchtower, an enormous granite pinnacle jutting out of the cliff. At 4 miles, the two trails rejoin. Stay to the left to the east end of Heather Lake. Continue north, crossing the outlet stream en route to the north end of the lake. This is the stopping point. Return to the junction with the Hump Trail and take the left fork. Switchbacks lead uphill through a lodgepole forest to The Hump. Descend 1,200 feet through a red fir forest, crossing a stream in a meadow. Complete the loop back at the junction with the Watchtower Trail. Bear left and retrace your steps, returning to the trailhead.

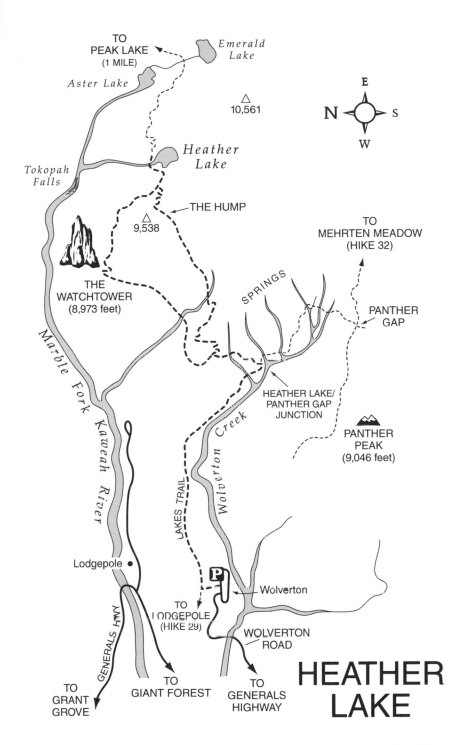

TO PEAK LAKE (1 MILE)

Emerald Lake

Aster Lake

△ 10,561

N E S W

Heather Lake

Tokopah Falls

THE HUMP

△ 9,538

TO MEHRTEN MEADOW (HIKE 32)

THE WATCHTOWER (8,973 feet)

SPRINGS

PANTHER GAP

HEATHER LAKE/ PANTHER GAP JUNCTION

Marble Fork Kaweah River

Wolverton Creek

PANTHER PEAK (9,046 feet)

LAKES TRAIL

Lodgepole ●

P

Wolverton

TO LODGEPOLE (HIKE 29)

WOLVERTON ROAD

GENERALS HWY

TO GRANT GROVE

TO GIANT FOREST

TO GENERALS HIGHWAY

HEATHER LAKE

Hike 32
Panther Gap and Mehrten Meadow

Hiking distance: 8 miles round trip
Hiking time: 4 hours
Elevation gain: 1,800 feet
Maps: U.S.G.S. Lodgepole
       Sequoia Natural History Assc.—Lodgepole/Wolverton

Summary of hike: This hike follows the Lakes Trail and Alta Trail to Panther Gap and Mehrten Meadow. Panther Gap sits on a ridge nearly 5,000 feet above the Middle Fork Kaweah River Canyon. The spectacular views include Castle Rocks and the 12,000-foot jagged peaks of the Great Western Divide. Mehrten Meadow is a small meadow tucked into a forested bowl alongside Mehrten Creek.

Driving directions: Follow the driving directions for Hike 30 to the Wolverton parking lot.

Hiking directions: Follow the hiking directions for the Lakes Trail along Wolverton Creek—Hike 30—to the Heather Lake/Panther Gap junction at 1.8 miles. Take the right fork towards Panther Gap. Cross a series of tributary streams of Wolverton Creek through an open fern-covered hillside. Leave the lush meadow, zigzagging up the steep slope through the red fir forest. At 2.8 miles, the trail reaches Panther Gap in a saddle on the ridge above the Middle Fork Kaweah River Canyon. From the 8,450-foot saddle are phenomenal views. This is a good destination for a shorter hike. To continue, bear left and head east on the Alta Trail. Follow the rocky edge of the cliffs above the deep canyon, reaching a trail split with the Sevenmile Hill Trail at 3.7 miles. (The right fork descends into the canyon, joining the High Sierra Trail.) Stay to the left, straight ahead into the forest on the Alta Trail. Curve downhill to Mehrten Creek and a few camp sites in Mehrten Meadow. Return along the same trail. To hike further, the trail continues up to Tharps Rock and Alta Peak at 11,200 feet, 2.6 miles ahead.

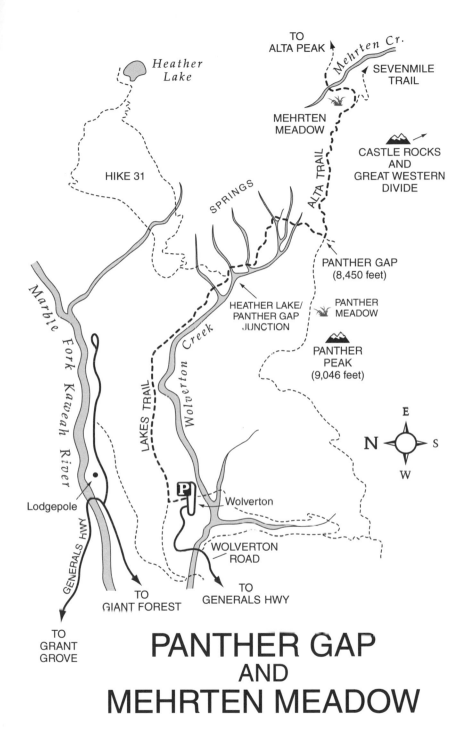

PANTHER GAP
AND
MEHRTEN MEADOW

Hike 33
Long Meadow Loop

Hiking distance: 2 mile loop
Hiking time: 1 hour
Elevation gain: 100 feet
Maps: U.S.G.S. Lodgepole
        Sequoia Natural History Assc.—Lodgepole/Wolverton

Summary of hike: Long Meadow was a Monache Indian village site during the summer. This hike circles the meadow through a forest of lodgepole and ponderosa pine, red fir and aspen trees. In the summer, the trail is also used as a horse trail by the Wolverton pack station. In the winter, it is a popular cross-country ski area.

Driving directions: The signed Wolverton turnoff is on the Generals Highway 1.6 miles southwest of Lodgepole and 2.5 miles north of Giant Forest Village. Drive 1.4 miles northeast on the Wolverton Road into the large Wolverton parking lot. Turn left and park in the lower south end of the lot by an unsigned path that leads to a rocky knoll.

Hiking directions: Take the narrow, unsigned footpath, crossing two culverts over Wolverton Creek. Climb up a small rocky knoll. Cross the trailless meadow 150 feet south, connecting with the well-defined Long Meadow Trail. Bear right, entering the dense forest. Wind through the shady canopy a short distance before breaking out into the open meadow. Follow the east edge of Long Meadow, darting in and out of the trees. Near the meadow's south end, two switchbacks lead up the hill. Cross a stream, and loop around the end of the meadow to a signed junction. The Alta Trail bears left up to Panther Gap (Hike 32). Stay to the right and head downhill through the forest along the west side of Long Meadow to the paved Wolverton Road. Bear right for 30 yards along the road, and pick up the footpath on the right. The footpath returns to the west end of the trailhead parking lot.

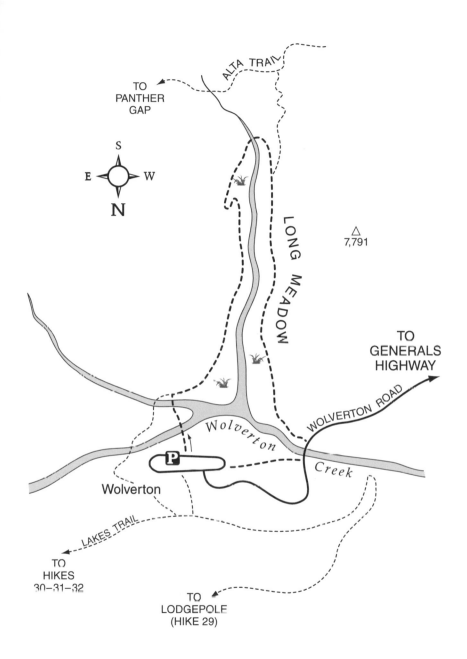

LONG MEADOW LOOP

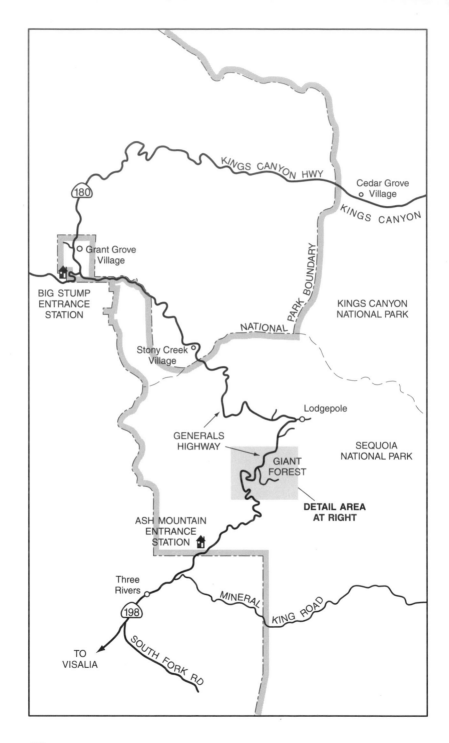

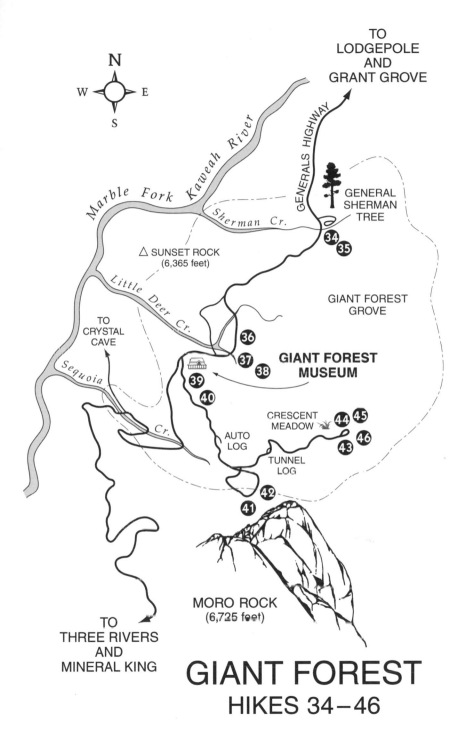

GIANT FOREST

HIKES 34–46

Hike 34
Congress Trail

Hiking distance: 2.1 mile loop
Hiking time: 1.5 hours
Elevation gain: 200 feet
Maps: U.S.G.S. Giant Forest and Lodgepole
      Sequoia Natural History Association—Giant Forest

Summary of hike: The Congress Trail is a premier hiking path through the heart of a sequoia grove in the Alta Plateau section of Giant Forest. It is a paved, handicapped accessible path beginning at the General Sherman Tree, the largest living organism on earth. The trail passes some of the finest stands of sequoias, including The President, General Lee, McKinley, Chief Sequoyah, and the House and Senate Groups.

Driving directions: The trailhead turnoff is on the east side of the Generals Highway 2.2 miles northeast of Giant Forest Museum at Crescent Meadow Road. Turn east at the signed General Sherman Tree parking lot and park in the lot

Hiking directions: Follow the signs on the paved path to the fenced General Sherman Tree. From the foot of the giant, follow the parking lot access road along the split-rail fence to the signed Congress Trail. Bear left, heading downhill towards Leaning Tree. Cross a footbridge over Sherman Creek, surrounded by the magnificent giants. Cross a second bridge over a branch of Sherman Creek, reaching a cut-off trail on the right at 0.5 miles. (Bear right for a shorter 0.8-mile loop.) Stay to the left and wind up the hillside to a four-way junction at 0.8 miles. Continue past the Alta Trail and the Trail of the Sequoias on the left (Hike 35). Stay on the paved Congress Trail past the Senate Group, a cluster of sequoias at another junction of the Trail of the Sequoias loop. Stay to the right past the House Group, reaching a junction at McKinley Tree. Take the right fork, weaving gradually downhill through the grove on the paved path. Cross over Sherman Creek, returning to the parking lot.

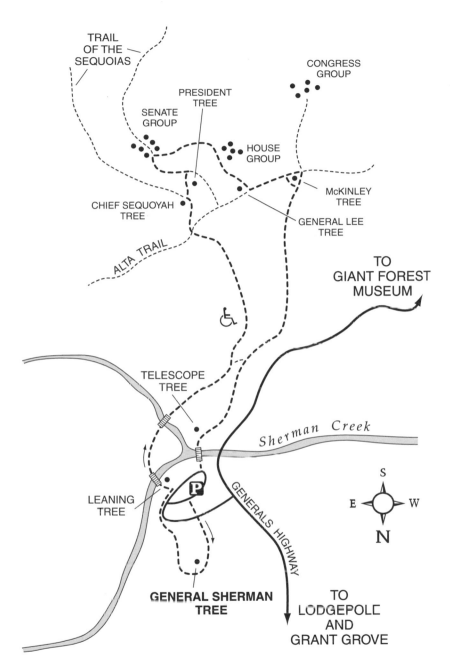

TRAIL OF THE SEQUOIAS

CONGRESS GROUP

PRESIDENT TREE

SENATE GROUP

HOUSE GROUP

CHIEF SEQUOYAH TREE

McKINLEY TREE

GENERAL LEE TREE

ALTA TRAIL

TO GIANT FOREST MUSEUM

TELESCOPE TREE

Sherman Creek

LEANING TREE

P

GENERALS HIGHWAY

S

E — W

N

GENERAL SHERMAN TREE

TO LODGEPOLE AND GRANT GROVE

CONGRESS TRAIL

Hike 35
Trail of the Sequoias

Hiking distance: 5.5 mile loop
Hiking time: 3 hours
Elevation gain: 500 feet
Maps: U.S.G.S. Giant Forest and Lodgepole
      Sequoia Natural History Association—Giant Forest

Summary of hike: This hike meanders through the Giant Forest Plateau in the relative solitude of a secluded forest among numerous stands of giant sequoias (back cover photo). The trail passes several meadows with creek crossings. The hike begins on the heavily used Congress Trail, but soon leads away from the crowds. At Log Meadow is Tharp's Log, a historic cabin with a stone fireplace built in a fire-hollowed sequoia. Every summer from 1861 through 1890, Hale Tharp lived in the hollow log while his cattle grazed in the meadows.

Driving directions: Follow the directions for Hike 34 to the General Sherman Tree parking lot.

Hiking directions: Take the signed Congress Trail at the east end of the parking area, and head downhill towards Leaning Tree. Surrounded by the magnificent giants, cross two foot-bridges over branches of Sherman Creek to a cut-off trail on the right at 0.5 miles. Stay to the left and wind up the hillside past the Alta Trail to the Trail of the Sequoias on the left. Leaving the paved Congress Trail, go left past the President and Chief Sequoyah Trees, winding through groves to a knoll at 1.5 miles. Descend past the headwaters of Crescent Creek and another cluster of giants. Pass through a fallen sequoia to a junction at 3 miles. Bear right and descend to a T-junction at Log Meadow. Stay to the right, and cross two forks of Crescent Creek to a junction at Tharp's Log at 3.3 miles. Take the right fork, climbing out of the meadow to Chimney Tree, a fire-hollowed tree. Stay to the right past two junctions at the north end of Crescent Meadow. Bear right again past a junction with the

Huckleberry Meadow Trail (Hike 38). Head uphill for a half mile, and take the right fork towards the Congress Trail. Follow the east side of Circle Meadow, rejoining the paved Congress Trail by the Senate Group. Bear left on the paved path to a junction at McKinley Tree. Take the right fork and weave through the grove back to the parking lot.

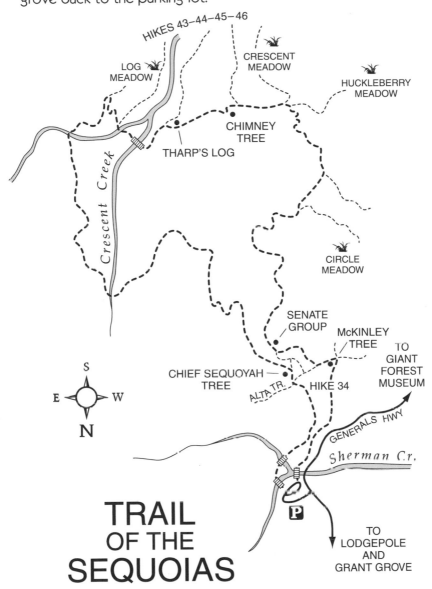

Hike 36
Rimrock—Alta Loop Trail

Hiking distance: 2.8 mile loop
Hiking time: 1.5 hours
Elevation gain: 400 feet
Maps: U.S.G.S. Giant Forest
Sequoia Natural History Association—Giant Forest

Summary of hike: The Rimrock Trail traverses a hillside ridge high above the Generals Highway past enormous granite rock formations and groves of giant sequoias. The return loop on the Alta Trail begins at Lincoln Tree, the fifth largest tree in the world. The trail passes bedrock mortars, cone-shaped holes in an exposed granite slab formed by Indians grinding acorns and pine nuts from the surrounding trees.

Driving directions: Park at the Hazelwood Nature Trail parking lot on the south side of the Generals Highway, 0.4 miles east of the Giant Forest Museum at Crescent Meadow Road.

Hiking directions: Follow the Hazelwood Nature Trail 0.1 mile to the first junction on the left. Take the left fork a hundred yards and bear right at a second junction. Cross the footbridge over a tributary of Little Deer Creek to another junction. Leave the nature loop and go left to the signed Rimrock Trail. Take the right fork 0.1 mile to a junction with the Alta Connector Trail, beginning the loop. Go straight ahead, staying on the Rimrock Trail. Cross an unpaved road at 0.7 miles. Curve to the right on the footpath, and traverse the hillside high above the Generals Highway. The path levels out in a lush sequoia grove. Meander among the giants to a signed T-junction at 1.7 miles by Lincoln Tree. Take the Alta Trail to the right, passing more clusters of sequoias. Stay to the right past two trail junctions. Cross Little Deer Creek to the bedrock mortars on an exposed granite slab to the right. At 2.2 miles is a signed junction. Leave the Alta Trail and descend on the right fork 0.3 miles, completing the loop. Bear left, back to the Hazelwood Nature Trail and trailhead.

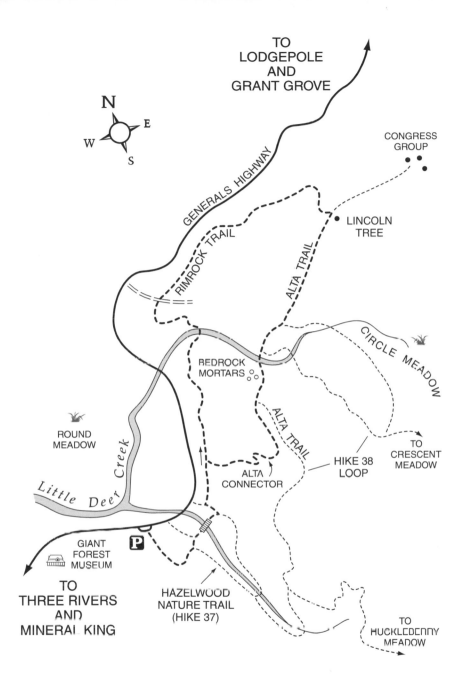

RIMROCK–ALTA LOOP

Hike 37
Hazelwood Nature Trail

Hiking distance: 1 mile loop
Hiking time: 30 minutes
Elevation gain: 100 feet
Maps: U.S.G.S. Giant Forest
       Sequoia Natural History Association—Giant Forest

Summary of hike: This nature loop is an easy stroll through a lush grove in Giant Forest. The trail meanders through majestic stands of giant sequoias with informative trailside exhibits. The exhibits describe the relationships and effects that fire and humans have had on the giant sequoias.

Driving directions: Park at the Hazelwood Nature Trail parking lot on the south side of the Generals Highway, 0.4 miles east of the Giant Forest Museum at Crescent Meadow Road.

Hiking directions: Follow the signed nature trail south, and walk through a fallen sequoia tree. Skirt past a moist, fern-filled grassy area on the right to a signed trail junction at a quarter mile. Stay to the right, beginning a counter-clockwise loop. At the south end of the nature trail is a junction. The right fork leads to Huckleberry Meadow on the Alta Trail (Hike 38). Bear left and begin the return loop. Head downhill, weaving through the grove to the north. Cross a wooden footbridge over a tributary stream of Little Deer Creek to a junction on the right. Stay to the left, completing the loop. Return to the trailhead to the right.

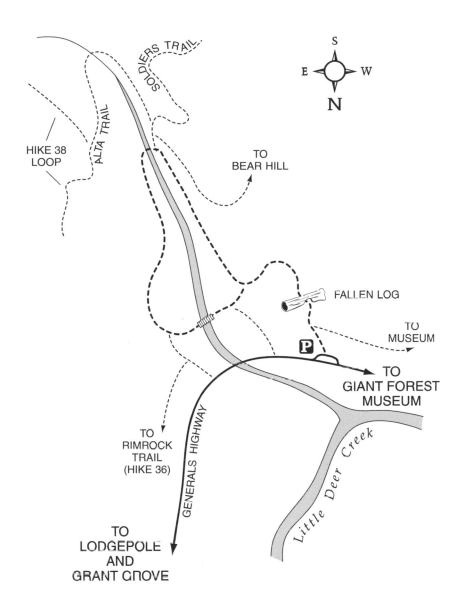

SOLDIERS TRAIL

ALTA TRAIL

HIKE 38
LOOP

S
E · W
N

TO
BEAR HILL

FALLEN LOG

TO
MUSEUM

P

TO
GIANT FOREST
MUSEUM

TO
RIMROCK
TRAIL
(HIKE 36)

GENERALS HIGHWAY

Little Deer Creek

TO
LODGEPOLE
AND
GRANT GROVE

HAZELWOOD
NATURE TRAIL

Hike 38
Huckleberry Meadow—Alta Trail Loop

Hiking distance: 4 mile loop
Hiking time: 2.5 hours
Elevation gain: 500 feet
Maps: U.S.G.S. Giant Forest
Sequoia Natural History Association—Giant Forest

Summary of hike: This loop hike begins on the Hazelwood Nature Trail (Hike 37) and circles through giant sequoia groves to the grassy wildflower-covered Huckleberry Meadow (cover photo). At the meadow is Squatter's Cabin, an 1880s one-room log cabin. The cabin was abandoned when the settler filed a land claim and discovered the land was already owned by Hale Tharp.

Driving directions: Follow the directions for Hike 37 to the Hazelwood Nature Trail parking lot.

Hiking directions: Head south on the Hazelwood Nature Trail to a junction at a quarter mile. Stay to the right to the south end of the nature loop. Take the right fork on the Alta Trail, heading uphill past junctions with the Bear Hill Trail (Hike 40) and Soldiers Trail (Hike 39). Begin the loop at the Huckleberry Trail at 0.7 miles. Take the right fork, climbing a steep hill through the forest to a ridge. At the ridge, the area becomes arid and devoid of sequoias. Descend back into a lush forest, plentiful with the giants, to Squatter's Cabin and a four-way junction at the northwest corner of Huckleberry Meadow. The right fork leads 0.2 miles to Dead Giant. The middle fork leads to the edge of Huckleberry Meadow. Take the left fork past more sequoias to a junction with the Trail of the Sequoias (Hike 35) at 2 miles. The right fork leads to Crescent Meadow (Hike 44). Go left, reaching another junction at 2.4 miles. Stay left, skirting Circle Meadow to Washington Tree (the second largest tree in the world) off a short spur trail. Continue to a junction with the Alta Trail at 3.2 miles. Go to the left, crossing Little Deer Creek to bedrock mortars, cone-shaped holes in an exposed granite slab formed by Indians grinding acorns and pine nuts. Just beyond the mortars is a junction.

Stay left on the Alta Trail, completing the loop. Go to the right back to the Hazelwood Nature Loop, and return to the trailhead.

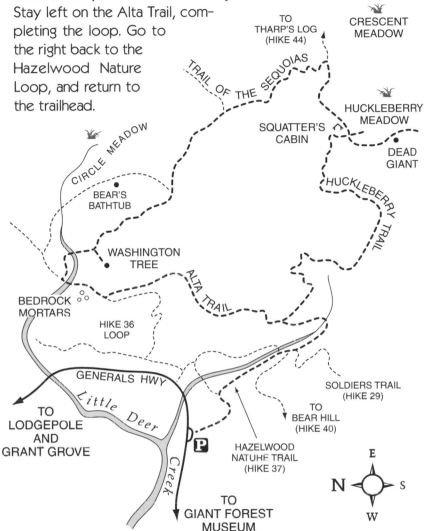

HUCKLEBERRY MEADOW
AND
ALTA TRAIL LOOP

Hike 39
Moro Rock—Soldiers Trail Loop

Hiking distance: 4.5 mile loop
Hiking time: 2.5 hours
Elevation gain: 400 feet
Maps: U.S.G.S. Giant Forest
Sequoia Natural History Association—Giant Forest

Summary of hike: This hike circles the west end of Giant Forest past numerous groves of giant sequoias, including Tunnel Log, Roosevelt Tree and Triple Tree. A short side path leads to Hanging Rock, a saucer-shaped boulder suspended on a large rock ledge overlooking the canyons of the Middle Fork and Marble Fork of the Kaweah River.

Driving directions: Park at the Giant Forest Museum parking lot on the Generals Highway at the northeast corner of Crescent Meadow Road.

Hiking directions: Walk 15 yards up Crescent Meadow Road to the signed Moro Rock Trail on the right (west) side of the road. Take the footpath uphill through the forest, parallel to Crescent Meadow Road. At 1.1 mile, the path curves right, reaching the Hanging Rock junction at Moro Rock Road. A short detour leads to Hanging Rock on the right. Return to the junction and follow the road 20 yards to the right, picking up the signed Moro Rock Trail on the left. Cross over the hill above the road 0.2 miles to a junction. The right fork descends to Moro Rock (Hike 41). Take the Soldiers Trail to the left. Switchbacks lead up to Roosevelt Tree and a signed junction. The Bear Hill Trail (Hike 40) forks to the left. Stay on the Soldiers Trail to the right, and descend past sequoias to Moro Rock Road by Triple Tree. Pick up the signed trail across the road, and walk around the base of Triple Tree, three sequoias fused together at the base. At 2.5 miles, cross Crescent Meadow Road on the west side of Tunnel Log. Continue through the forest past the historic site of Soldiers Camp Meadow, a U.S. Cavalry camp used in

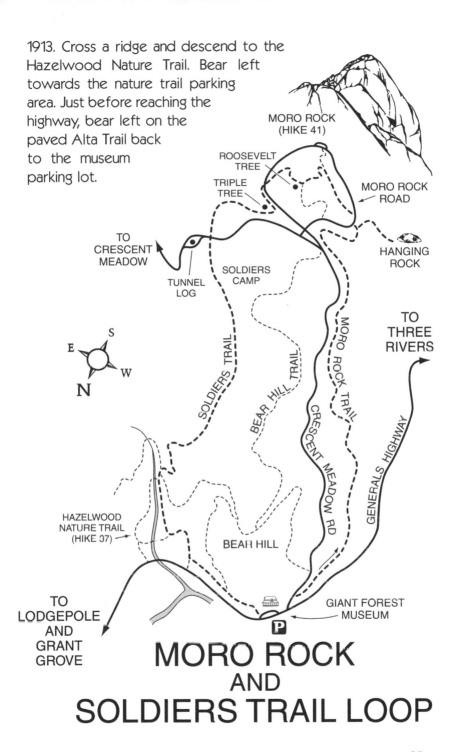

1913. Cross a ridge and descend to the Hazelwood Nature Trail. Bear left towards the nature trail parking area. Just before reaching the highway, bear left on the paved Alta Trail back to the museum parking lot.

MORO ROCK
(HIKE 41)

ROOSEVELT
TREE

TRIPLE
TREE

MORO ROCK
ROAD

TO
CRESCENT
MEADOW

SOLDIERS
CAMP

HANGING
ROCK

TUNNEL
LOG

S

E   W

N

SOLDIERS TRAIL

BEAR HILL TRAIL

MORO ROCK TRAIL

CRESCENT MEADOW RD

GENERALS HIGHWAY

TO
THREE
RIVERS

HAZELWOOD
NATURE TRAIL
(HIKE 37)

BEAR HILL

TO
LODGEPOLE
AND
GRANT
GROVE

GIANT FOREST
MUSEUM

P

MORO ROCK
AND
SOLDIERS TRAIL LOOP

Hike 40
Bear Hill Trail

Hiking distance: 4 miles round trip
Hiking time: 2 hours
Elevation gain: 200 feet
Maps: U.S.G.S. Giant Forest
        Sequoia Natural History Association—Giant Forest

Summary of hike: During the 1920s and 1930s, Bear Hill was a garbage dump site (and feeding ground) for black bears. It was closed in the 1940s due to conflicts between bears and humans. This hike crosses Bear Hill past giant sequoias, connecting with the Soldiers Trail near Moro Rock.

Driving directions: Park at the Giant Forest Museum parking lot on the Generals Highway at the northeast corner of Crescent Meadow Road.

Hiking directions: Walk 0.1 mile up Crescent Meadow Road to the signed Bear Hill Trail on the left. Head up the hillside on the wide trail, following a portion of the original park road replaced by the Generals Highway. At 0.5 miles, the trail reaches a knoll and signed junction at the base of Bear Hill. The left fork leads to the Hazelwood Nature Trail (Hike 37) and the Alta Trail. Bear to the right along the west flank of Bear Hill. The near level trail winds through a forest of sugar pines, white firs and giant sequoias, reaching another knoll at 1.5 miles. Descend to Crescent Meadow Road at a Y-fork. Take the right fork of the road, and go right again on the Moro Rock Road, picking up the signed trail on the left. Wind up the hillside to the end of the Bear Hill Trail at Roosevelt Tree and a signed junction. The right fork descends to Moro Rock (Hike 41) and Hanging Rock. The Soldiers Trail (Hike 39) goes to the left. All three routes return to the museum and trailhead.

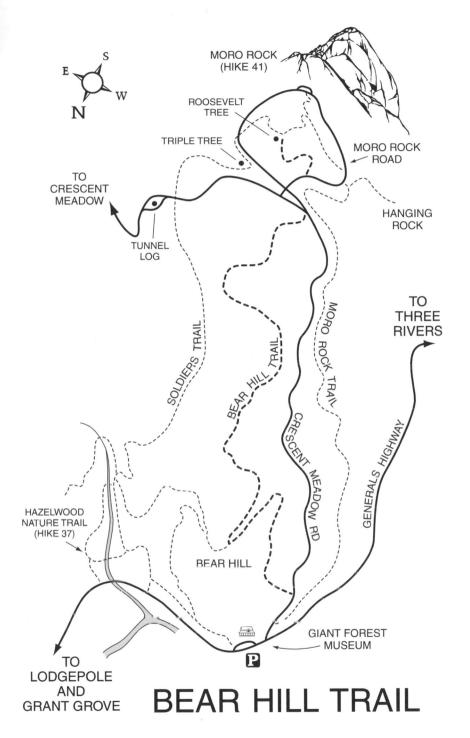

MORO ROCK
(HIKE 41)

ROOSEVELT
TREE

TRIPLE TREE

MORO ROCK
ROAD

TO
CRESCENT
MEADOW

HANGING
ROCK

TUNNEL
LOG

TO
THREE
RIVERS

SOLDIERS TRAIL

BEAR HILL TRAIL

MORO ROCK TRAIL

CRESCENT MEADOW RD

GENERALS HIGHWAY

HAZELWOOD
NATURE TRAIL
(HIKE 37)

BEAR HILL

GIANT FOREST
MUSEUM

TO
LODGEPOLE
AND
GRANT GROVE

S

E

W

N

BEAR HILL TRAIL

Hike 41
Moro Rock

Hiking distance: 0.6 miles round trip
Hiking time: 30 minutes
Elevation gain: 300 feet
Maps: U.S.G.S. Giant Forest
        Sequoia Natural History Association—Giant Forest

Summary of hike: This hike climbs to the top of Moro Rock at its 6,725-foot summit. The prominent, oblong granite dome juts out from the 4,000-foot canyon wall at the edge of the Giant Forest Plateau. Atop the massive monolith are awesome panoramic views that include the canyons of the Middle Fork and Marble Fork of the Kaweah River, the serpentine Generals Highway snaking its way down to the foothills, the scalloped ridge of the Great Western Divide, the 9,081-foot jagged spires of Castle Rocks, the Giant Forest Plateau and the San Joaquin Valley. The trail has interpretive displays about the geologic and human history, including a map at the summit identifying the many distant peaks and valleys.

Driving directions: From Generals Highway and Crescent Meadow Road by the Giant Forest Museum, drive 1.2 miles on Crescent Meadow Road to the Moro Rock turnoff. Turn right and continue 0.4 miles to the paved Moro Rock parking lot on the right.

Hiking directions: Immediately begin climbing south on Moro Rock itself. The trail twists up the spine of the imposing rock, climbing 380 granite stairs built in 1931. Continue up switchbacks, rock slab ramps and landings to the summit, perched on the ridgetop. Metal railings line portions of the steep trail as an aid. Along the way are frequent overlooks and trailside exhibits. The summit is enclosed by railings. After savoring the views and identifying the various peaks and features, return along the only path.

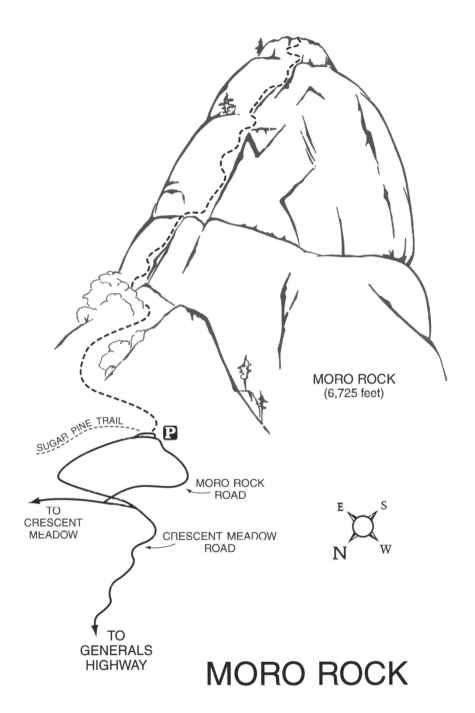

MORO ROCK
(6,725 feet)

SUGAR PINE TRAIL

P

MORO ROCK
ROAD

TO
CRESCENT
MEADOW

CRESCENT MEADOW
ROAD

TO
GENERALS
HIGHWAY

E S
N W

MORO ROCK

Hike 42
Sugar Pine Trail

Hiking distance: 3 miles round trip
Hiking time: 1.5 hours
Elevation gain: 300 feet
Maps: U.S.G.S. Giant Forest and Lodgepole
      Sequoia Natural History Association—Giant Forest

Summary of hike: The Sugar Pine Trail connects Moro Rock with Crescent Meadow along the edge of the Middle Fork Kaweah River Canyon. Views extend up and down the canyon, including the sculpted spires of Castle Rocks and the jagged peaks of the Great Western Divide. The path crosses two groups of Indian mortar holes, cone-shaped holes in the rocks formed by Indians grinding acorns and pine nuts into meal.

Driving directions: From Generals Highway and Crescent Meadow Road by the Giant Forest Museum, drive 1.2 miles on Crescent Meadow Road to the Moro Rock turnoff. Turn right and continue 0.4 miles to the paved Moro Rock parking lot on the right.

Hiking directions: The signed trail begins to the left (east) side of Moro Rock. Head sharply downhill, dropping one hundred feet on the well-defined path. Curve along the forested north slope of the canyon, following the contours of the hillside to a signed junction at 1.2 miles. The right fork crosses Crescent Creek by pools etched in the bowl-shaped contours of the rock. Continue straight ahead on the left fork parallel to Crescent Creek. A short distance ahead, the path crosses a large flat slab of rock. Detour to the left and climb the rock mound to a sign at the bedrock mortars. Return to the main trail and continue east, following Crescent Creek to more bedrock mortars on the right. Wind through the forest, reaching the Crescent Meadow parking lot. This is our turnaround spot.

To hike further, several trails begin from the Crescent Meadow parking lot, including hikes 43—46.

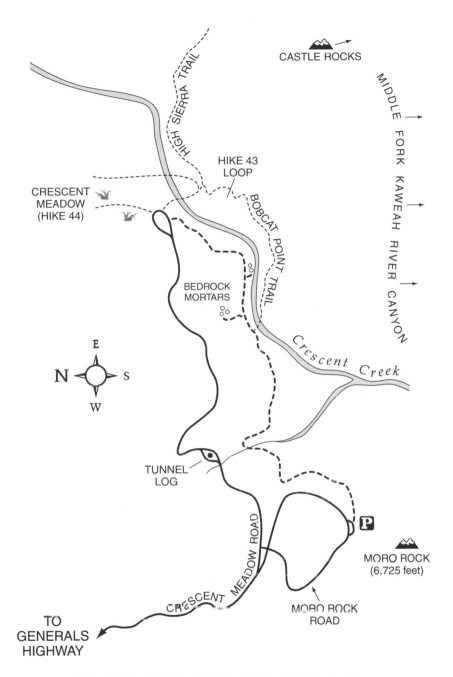

CASTLE ROCKS

HIGH SIERRA TRAIL

HIKE 43 LOOP

MIDDLE FORK KAWEAH RIVER CANYON

CRESCENT MEADOW (HIKE 44)

BOBCAT POINT TRAIL

BEDROCK MORTARS

Crescent Creek

N E S W

TUNNEL LOG

P

MORO ROCK (6,725 feet)

CRESCENT MEADOW ROAD

MORO ROCK ROAD

TO GENERALS HIGHWAY

SUGAR PINE TRAIL

Hike 43
Bobcat Point Loop

Hiking distance: 1.2 mile loop
Hiking time: 40 minutes
Elevation gain: 200 feet
Maps: U.S.G.S. Giant Forest and Lodgepole
Sequoia Natural History Association—Giant Forest

Summary of hike: This hike leads to Kaweah Vista and Bobcat Point, two stunning overlooks on the rim of the 3,000-foot deep Middle Fork Kaweah River canyon. On the return, the hike crosses two groups of bedrock mortars, where Indians ground acorns and seeds into meal.

Driving directions: From Generals Highway and Crescent Meadow Road by the Giant Forest Museum, drive 2.6 miles to the end of Crescent Meadow Road, bearing left at the Moro Rock road fork. Park in the paved parking lot at the road's end.

Hiking directions: Take the paved High Sierra Trail from the east end of the parking area. Loop around the south end of Crescent Meadow, crossing two wooden footbridges over Crescent Creek to a signed junction. The paved left fork circles Crescent Meadow (Hike 44). Stay on the High Sierra Trail to a second junction 20 yards ahead. The left fork leads to Eagle View (Hike 46). Take the signed right fork towards Moro Rock. Head up the forested hill to the ridge overlooking the Middle Fork Kaweah River canyon. Parallel the edge of the canyon to Kaweah Vista, a rock outcrop on the canyon rim. Continue a short distance to Bobcat Point, an overlook at a second rock outcrop. Leave the edge of the canyon, and descend to a large flat slab of granite rock at Crescent Creek. Pools sit in the bowl-shaped contours of the rock. Cross the creek to a T-junction with the Sugar Pine Trail (Hike 42). The left fork leads to Moro Rock. Bear right parallel to Crescent Creek, reaching a large rock slab on the left. Leave the trail temporarily, and climb the rock mound to the Indian mortars and an interpretive sign. Return to the main trail and continue east, following Crescent Creek upstream to a second set of Indian mortars on the right. Wind through the forest back to the south end of the parking lot.

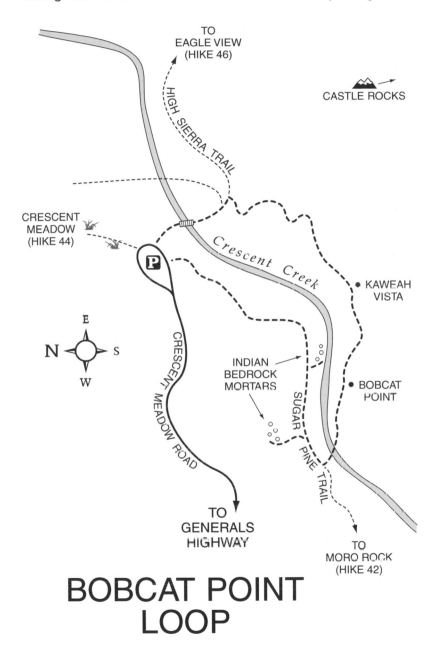

TO
EAGLE VIEW
(HIKE 46)

HIGH SIERRA TRAIL

CASTLE ROCKS

CRESCENT
MEADOW
(HIKE 44)

P

Crescent Creek

KAWEAH
VISTA

E
N S
W

CRESCENT MEADOW ROAD

INDIAN
BEDROCK
MORTARS

SUGAR PINE TRAIL

BOBCAT
POINT

TO
GENERALS
HIGHWAY

TO
MORO ROCK
(HIKE 42)

BOBCAT POINT LOOP

Hike 44
Crescent Meadow Loop

Hiking distance: 1.75 mile loop
Hiking time: 1 hour
Elevation gain: 150 feet
Maps: U.S.G.S. Giant Forest and Lodgepole
       Sequoia Natural History Association—Giant Forest

Summary of hike: Crescent Meadow is a stream-fed, flower-filled meadow rimmed with firs and giant sequoias. It is one of the most picturesque meadows in the park. This hike links several paths, forming a loop through groves of giant sequoias. The hike leads to Tharp's Log, a pioneer's home built inside a fallen giant sequoia. Hale Tharp lived here during the summers from 1861 to 1890, pasturing his cattle in the meadows.

Driving directions: From Generals Highway and Crescent Meadow Road by the Giant Forest Museum, drive 2.6 miles to the end of Crescent Meadow Road, bearing left at the Moro Rock road fork. Park in the paved parking lot at the road's end.

Hiking directions: Take the paved High Sierra Trail from the east end of the parking lot. Cross two wooden footbridges over Crescent Creek to a signed junction. The right fork follows the High Sierra Trail (Hike 46). Take the paved trail to the left, rounding the southern end of Crescent Meadow. Cross a bridge over Crescent Creek to a signed junction. The left fork follows Crescent Meadow towards the Cleveland Tree. Leave Crescent Meadow for now, and begin the loop to the right towards Tharp's Log. A short distance ahead is a signed junction with the Log Meadow Loop (Hike 45). Go left through the dense fir forest, skirting the west edge of Log Meadow to a junction at Tharp's Log. Bear left, climbing out of the meadow basin. Continue past Chimney Tree to the second signed Crescent Meadow junction at the northwest side of the meadow. Bear left, heading south through the forest while skirting the meadow. The paved path returns to the picnic area at the parking lot.

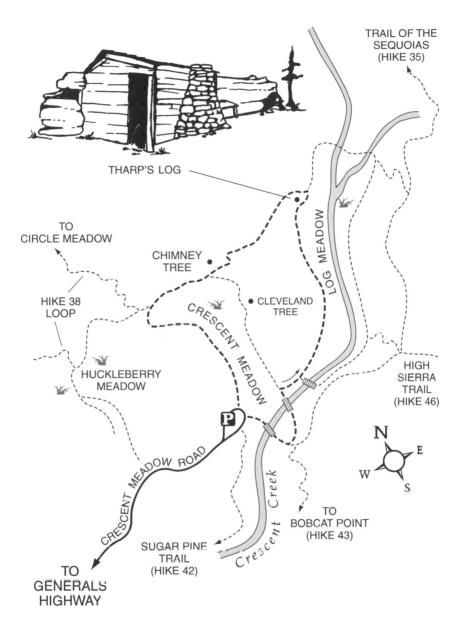

TRAIL OF THE
SEQUOIAS
(HIKE 35)

THARP'S LOG

TO
CIRCLE MEADOW

CHIMNEY
TREE

CLEVELAND
TREE

HIKE 38
LOOP

LOG MEADOW

CRESCENT MEADOW

HUCKLEBERRY
MEADOW

HIGH
SIERRA
TRAIL
(HIKE 46)

P

CRESCENT MEADOW ROAD

Crescent Creek

N
E
W
S

TO
BOBCAT POINT
(HIKE 43)

SUGAR PINE
TRAIL
(HIKE 42)

TO
GENERALS
HIGHWAY

CRESCENT MEADOW
LOOP

Hike 45
Log Meadow Loop

Hiking distance: 2.3 mile loop
Hiking time: 1.5 hours
Elevation gain: 150 feet
Maps: U.S.G.S. Lodgepole
　　　　Sequoia Natural History Association—Giant Forest

Summary of hike: Log Meadow is a lush grassy meadow carpeted with flowers and surrounded by giant sequoias. At the north end of the meadow is Tharp's Log, a pioneer's summer home built in a fire-hollowed fallen sequoia. Hale Tharp lived in the hollow log from 1861 to 1890, pasturing his cattle in these meadows. This hike loops around Log Meadow, linking several interconnecting paths.

Driving directions: From Generals Highway and Crescent Meadow Road by the Giant Forest Museum, drive 2.6 miles to the end of Crescent Meadow Road, bearing left at the Moro Rock road fork. Park in the paved parking lot at the road's end.

Hiking directions: Take the paved High Sierra Trail from the east end of the parking lot. Cross two wooden footbridges over Crescent Creek to a signed junction. The right fork follows the High Sierra Trail (Hike 46). Take the paved trail to the left, rounding the southern end of Crescent Meadow. Cross a wooden bridge over Crescent Creek to a signed junction. (The left fork follows Crescent Meadow towards the Cleveland Tree.) Leave Crescent Meadow and go to the right towards Tharp's Log. In a short distance is the junction that begins the Log Meadow Loop. Go left, following the trail through the dense fir forest along the west side of Log Meadow to Tharp's Log. The left fork leads to Chimney Tree and returns to Crescent Meadow (Hike 44). Go to the right, looping around the north end of Log Meadow. Cross two forks of Crescent Creek to a junction. The left fork connects with the Trail of the Sequoias (Hike 35). Continue on the right fork along the east edge of Log

Meadow towards the High Sierra Trail. Curve to the right at the next junction and cross a footbridge over the meadow outlet stream, completing the loop. Take the left fork and return to the trailhead around the south end of Crescent Meadow.

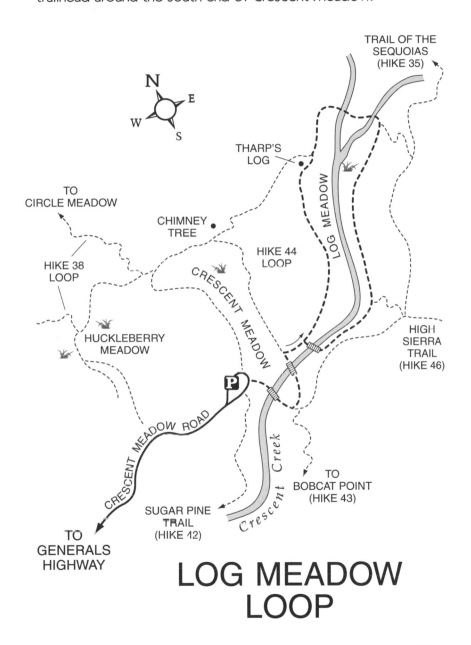

LOG MEADOW LOOP

Hike 46
High Sierra Trail to Eagle View

Hiking distance: 1.5 miles round trip
Hiking time: 1 hour
Elevation gain: 100 feet
Maps: U.S.G.S. Lodgepole
      Sequoia Natural History Association—Giant Forest

Summary of hike: The High Sierra Trail is a trans-Sierra back-packing route. It leads 34 miles to the Kern River Canyon and 71 miles to the summit of Mount Whitney at 14,495 feet, the highest peak in the contiguous United States. This hike takes the first 0.75 miles of the High Sierra Trail from Crescent Meadow to Eagle View. The trail follows the northern rim of the Middle Fork Kaweah River canyon. From Eagle View are expansive 180-degree views of the 3,000-foot deep canyon. The vistas include Moro Rock, Castle Rocks and the pointed summits of the Great Western Divide.

Driving directions: From Generals Highway and Crescent Meadow Road by the Giant Forest Museum, drive 2.6 miles to the end of Crescent Meadow Road, bearing left at the Moro Rock road fork. Park in the paved parking lot at the road's end.

Hiking directions: From the east end of the parking lot, take the signed High Sierra Trail on the paved path. Loop around the south end of Crescent Meadow, crossing two wooden footbridges over Crescent Creek to a signed junction. The paved left fork circles Crescent Meadow. Stay on the High Sierra Trail to the right to a second junction 20 yards ahead. The right fork leads to Bobcat Point. Stay to the left, gently winding uphill through the forest to a signed four-way junction at 0.6 miles. The sharp left fork descends to Log Meadow. The middle route connects with the Trail of the Sequoias. Bear to the right, following the rim of the deep Middle Fork Kaweah River canyon. An interpretive display describes the effects of the 1988 Buckeye Fire that burned over 3,100 acres, which can be seen below. Follow the edge of the cliffs to Eagle View. After savoring the views, return along the same trail.

To hike further, the trail continues along the edge of the cliffs for several miles, crossing a series of tributary streams of Panther Creek.

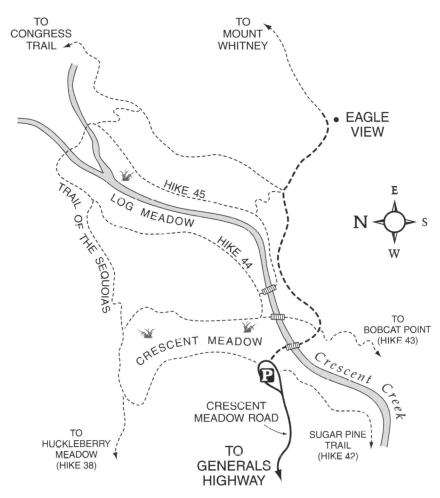

HIGH SIERRA TRAIL
TO
EAGLE VIEW

Hike 47
Middle Fork Trail to Panther Creek Falls

Hiking distance: 6 miles round trip
Hiking time: 3 hours
Elevation gain: 600 feet
Maps: U.S.G.S. Giant Forest and Lodgepole

Summary of hike: Panther Creek Falls plunges a hundred feet off massive granite boulders and continues down the cliffs into the Middle Fork of the Kaweah River. The Middle Fork Trail traverses the Middle Fork Canyon on a cliff-hugging path along the steep north canyon wall. The path alternates from exposed chaparral to shady, forested nooks with stream-fed rock grottos. The journey up canyon provides broad views of the upper Middle Fork Canyon, Alta Peak and the Great Western Divide.

Driving directions: From the Ash Mountain entrance, drive 6 miles north on the Generals Highway to the Buckeye Campground turnoff and turn right. Drive a half mile on the winding campground road to a road split. Bear left and continue 1.3 miles on the unpaved road to the signed trailhead parking area at the road's end. During the winter, the campground road is closed so park in the Hospital Rock parking lot on the left, across the road from the Buckeye Campground turnoff. This will add 3.6 miles round trip to the hike.

Hiking directions: Head east on the signed footpath for a hundred yards to a hidden recess at Moro Creek by a beautiful pool and a cascade over granite slabs. Rock hop over the creek, and head uphill on the treeless slope under the shadow of Moro Rock. Throughout the hike, notice the ever-changing views of the Castle Rocks across the canyon. Curve in and out from shady ravines to exposed ledges along the contours of the canyon. The trail remains more than 200 feet above the Middle Fork of the Kaweah River. At 3 miles, a short, steep descent leads to the top of Panther Creek Falls among pines and cedars. After resting on boulders by the falls and viewing the canyon and river below, return on the same path.

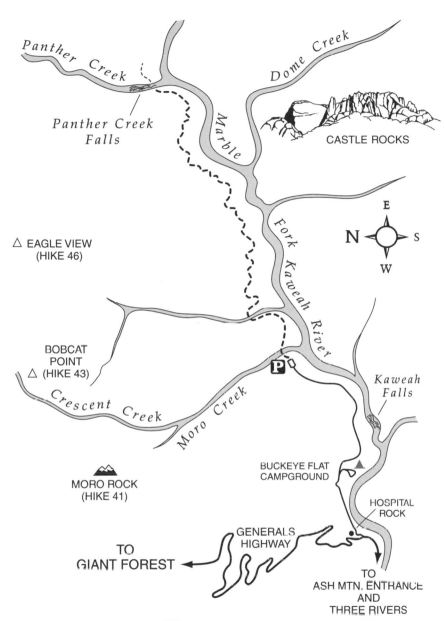

Panther Creek

Panther Creek Falls

Marble

Dome Creek

CASTLE ROCKS

Fork Kaweah River

△ EAGLE VIEW (HIKE 46)

BOBCAT POINT △ (HIKE 43)

Crescent Creek

Moro Creek

Kaweah Falls

MORO ROCK (HIKE 41)

BUCKEYE FLAT CAMPGROUND

HOSPITAL ROCK

GENERALS HIGHWAY

TO GIANT FOREST

TO ASH MTN. ENTRANCE AND THREE RIVERS

MIDDLE FORK TRAIL
TO
PANTHER CREEK FALLS

Hike 48
Middle Fork Kaweah Falls from Hospital Rock

Hiking distance: 1.6 miles round trip
Hiking time: 1 hour
Elevation gain: 150 feet
Maps: U.S.G.S. Giant Forest

Summary of hike: Middle Fork Kaweah Falls is a wide, powerful 20-foot high cataract on the Middle Fork Kaweah River. At the base of the falls is an enormous pool surrounded by multi-colored polished rock formations. There are numerous flat rocks to sit on and view the falls.

Driving directions: From the Ash Mountain entrance, drive 6 miles north on the Generals Highway, and park in the Hospital Rock parking lot on the left. The parking lot is located across from the Buckeye Campground turnoff on the right. Trailhead parking is not allowed from the campground. Unless you are camped at Buckeye Campground, begin the hike from Hospital Rock, 0.6 miles from the trailhead.

Hiking directions: Cross the highway to Hospital Rock by the Indian bedrock mortars and pictographs. Hike up the canyon on the oak-lined Buckeye Campground Road. The road follows the contours of the canyon, overlooking the Middle Fork Kaweah River and Castle Rocks. At 0.5 miles is a road split. The left fork leads to the Middle Fork Trail (Hike 47). Take the right fork and descend into the Buckeye Campground. Bear left 20 yards to the signed trail on the left, across from campsite 28. Take the footpath up the hillside, quickly reaching pools and small waterfalls by a footbridge. Cross the 40-foot bridge over the Middle Fork Kaweah River to a four-way junction. The path to the right heads downstream to a beautiful olympic-size pool. The middle path leads to Paradise Creek (Hike 49). Go left, heading upstream past more pools and large boulders. A short distance ahead are the waterfall, pool and gorgeous rock formations. The path continues beyond the falls to additional pools.

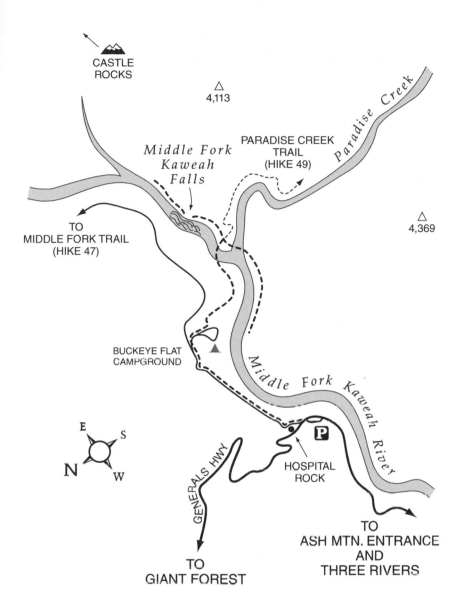

CASTLE
ROCKS

△
4,113

*Middle Fork
Kaweah
Falls*

PARADISE CREEK
TRAIL
(HIKE 49)

Paradise Creek

TO
MIDDLE FORK TRAIL
(HIKE 47)

△
4,369

BUCKEYE FLAT
CAMPGROUND

Middle Fork Kaweah River

E S
N W

GENERALS HWY

P

HOSPITAL
ROCK

TO
GIANT FOREST

TO
ASH MTN. ENTRANCE
AND
THREE RIVERS

KAWEAH FALLS
FROM
HOSPITAL ROCK

Hike 49
Paradise Creek Trail from Hospital Rock

Hiking distance: 3.6 miles round trip
Hiking time: 2 hours
Elevation gain: 550 feet
Maps: U.S.G.S. Giant Forest

Summary of hike: The Paradise Creek Trail crosses a 40-foot bridge over the Middle Fork Kaweah River by pools, cascades and waterfalls. It leaves the river canyon and follows Paradise Creek up a lush, narrow side canyon. From Paradise Canyon are impressive views across the Middle Fork Canyon to Moro Rock and Bobcat Point.

Driving directions: Follow the driving directions for Hike 48 to the Hospital Rock parking lot.

Hiking directions: Follow the hiking directions for Hike 48 to the four-way trail junction just after the wooden bridge. At the junction, paths lead up and down the south banks of the river. Take the middle path, following a water pipe for 20 yards through an oak grove to a trail split. Bear left to more pools and cascades in a narrow rock canyon. Switchbacks lead up the hillside away from but parallel to Paradise Creek. Follow the ridge between Paradise Creek and the Middle Fork Kaweah River through a shady oak grove. Traverse the east cliffs up the narrow canyon overlooking the creek. The path curves sharply to the right, crossing a lush ravine. Head deeper up canyon past more pools and cascades, reaching the creek in an oak woodland. Continue back up the hillside past mossy rocks to a creek crossing by pools at 1.7 miles. Follow the west bank of the creek for 0.1 mile and recross. After the second crossing the trail becomes faint and is not maintained. Return along the same path.

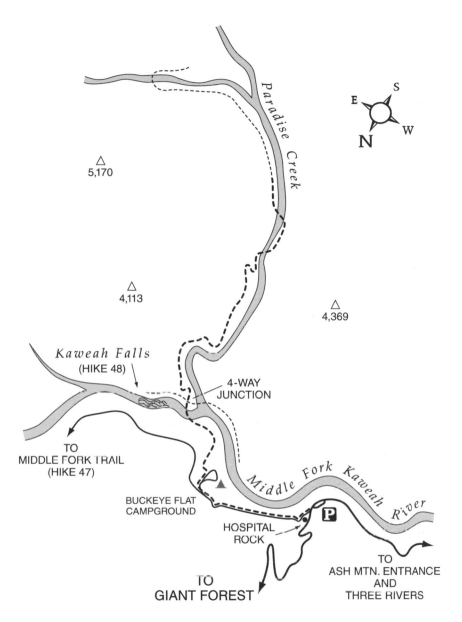

PARADISE CREEK TRAIL
FROM
HOSPITAL ROCK

Hike 50
Middle Fork Trail
Hospital Rock to Potwisha Campground

Hiking distance: 5 miles round trip
Hiking time: 2.5 hours
Elevation gain: 700 feet
Maps: U.S.G.S. Giant Forest

Summary of hike: This hike follows an ancient foothills trail that linked two Indian village sites. The trail parallels the Middle Fork Kaweah River from Hospital Rock to the Potwisha Campground. The path follows the north canyon wall on a shelf that hugs the hillside. The terrain varies from grass and chaparral to an oak woodland.

Driving directions: From the Ash Mountain entrance, drive 6 miles north on the Generals Highway, and park in the Hospital Rock parking lot on the left. The parking lot is located across from the Buckeye Campground turnoff on the right.

Hiking directions: Walk across the picnic area to the signed trailhead at the edge of the hillside below the water tank. Bear left and head east through the oak woodland. Traverse the hillside along the north canyon wall with views of Moro Rock, Castle Rocks and the cascading Middle Fork Kaweah River. At 1.5 miles, switchbacks lead down to the Generals Highway. Cross the road and wind down the footpath above and parallel to the river. The trail descends to the Potwisha RV dump station, across the road from the Potwisha Campground. The dump station is also the trailhead to the Potwisha Pictographs and Hanging Bridge (Hike 52). The trail to Marble Falls (Hike 51) begins across the road in the campground. To return, take the same trail back to Hospital Rock.

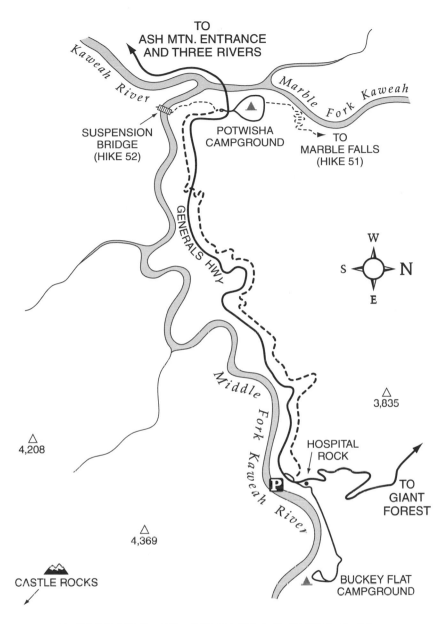

TO
ASH MTN. ENTRANCE
AND THREE RIVERS

Kaweah River

Marble Fork Kaweah

SUSPENSION
BRIDGE
(HIKE 52)

POTWISHA
CAMPGROUND

TO
MARBLE FALLS
(HIKE 51)

GENERALS HWY

W
S ● N
E

Middle Fork Kaweah River

△
3,835

HOSPITAL
ROCK

△
4,208

P

TO
GIANT
FOREST

△
4,369

CASTLE ROCKS

BUCKEY FLAT
CAMPGROUND

MIDDLE FORK TRAIL
TO
POTWISHA CAMPGROUND

Hike 51
Marble Fork Trail to Marble Falls

Hiking distance: 7 mile round trip
Hiking time: 3.5 hours
Elevation gain: 1,500 feet
Maps: U.S.G.S. Giant Forest

Summary of hike: Marble Falls is a series of powerful whitewater cascades over beautiful multicolored marble on the Marble Fork Kaweah River. This trail parallels the river up canyon, traversing the chaparral-clad slopes. The hike passes marble outcroppings en route to the deep gorge at Marble Falls.

Driving directions: From the Ash Mountain entrance, drive 3.8 miles north on the Generals Highway to the Potwisha Campground and turn left. Drive 0.3 miles around the one-way campground loop to the signed trail on the right by campsite 16. Turn right and park in the spaces by the trailhead.

Hiking directions: Walk north up the wide gravel path through an oak woodland to a trail split. The left fork leads downhill to pools and cascades on the Marble Fork Kaweah River. Bear right, crossing a bridge over a concrete aquaduct. A hundred yards ahead by a water gate is the signed trail on the right. Short, steep switchbacks lead up the hillside through an oak forest. The grade becomes moderate and follows the contours of the mountain ridges. The trail emerges from the forest at 1.2 miles and gives way to the dry and exposed chaparral-covered hillside. Continue north on the narrow path along the steep east canyon wall. The trail curves in and out from sunny slopes to lush, shady stream-fed nooks. Several hundred feet below, the whitewater of the Marble Fork Kaweah River is visible. Near Marble Falls, the path passes marble outcroppings and descends to an overlook of the cataract. Drop down to the river's edge at the bottom of the rocky gorge by the falls. The trail ends here. Hiking up or down river is dangerous and not recommended. Return along the same trail.

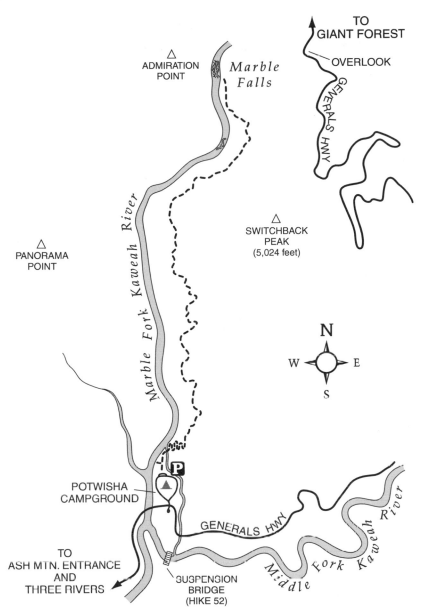

TO
GIANT FOREST

OVERLOOK

GENERALS HWY

△
ADMIRATION
POINT

*Marble
Falls*

△
SWITCHBACK
PEAK
(5,024 feet)

Marble Fork Kaweah River

△
PANORAMA
POINT

N
W E
S

P

POTWISHA
CAMPGROUND

GENERALS HWY

Middle Fork Kaweah River

TO
ASH MTN. ENTRANCE
AND
THREE RIVERS

SUSPENSION
BRIDGE
(HIKE 52)

MIDDLE FORK TRAIL
TO
MARBLE FALLS

Hike 52
Potwisha Pictographs and Suspension Bridge

Hiking distance: 1 mile round trip
Hiking time: 30 minutes
Elevation gain: 100 feet
Maps: U.S.G.S. Giant Forest

Summary of hike: This hike leads to an area by the Middle Fork Kaweah River that was once a Monache Indian village site. Bedrock mortars, formed by Indians grinding acorns and nuts into meal, and pictographs on a large overhanging rock, still remain. At the river are beautiful cascades over smooth rock, forming a series of pools. A suspension bridge spans the river by sculpted rocks and a sandy beach.

Driving directions: From the Ash Mountain entrance, drive 3.8 miles north on the Generals Highway to the Potwisha Campground on the left. Turn to the right, across from the campground entrance, towards the RV dump station on the paved road. Continue 0.2 miles, bearing to the right, and park in the lot at the end of the road.

Hiking directions: The trail begins on the left side of the parking area. A short distance beyond the trailhead is a trail split. Take the left fork about 100 feet where you will begin spotting the bedrock mortars along a large slab of exposed granite. Continue to the Indian pictographs on the large rock hanging over the trail from the left. The drawings can be seen on the underside of the rock. Continue past the rock to an unsigned junction. The left fork leads to Hospital Rock on an ancient Indian route (Hike 50). Turn right, down to the Middle Fork Kaweah River and the 100-foot suspension bridge. Cross the bridge to a sandy beach on the right and sculpted rocks, cascades and pools up and down the river. After exploring, recross the bridge and take the trail to the left alongside the river. Follow the trail downstream and complete the loop, returning left to the trailhead.

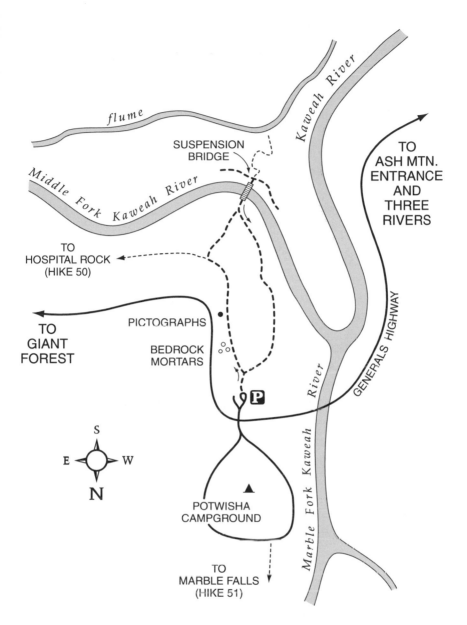

POTWISHA PICTOGRAPHS
AND
SUSPENSION BRIDGE

Hike 53
Indian Head Trail to Kaweah River

Hiking distance: 0.4 miles round trip
Hiking time: 30 minutes
Elevation gain: 100 feet
Maps: U.S.G.S. Case Mountain

Summary of hike: The Indian Head Trail is a short hike to a spectacular, large pool and a series of smaller pools on the Kaweah River. Rock steps lead to terraces of smooth, water-sculpted rocks perfect for sitting and sunbathing.

Driving directions: From the Ash Mountain entrance, drive 0.1 mile north to the parking lot on the right. There is a carved redwood Indian head sign announcing "Sequoia National Park" at the parking lot.

Hiking directions: The trail begins near the center of the parking lot and heads south. The well-defined path leads downhill towards the Kaweah River. Moro Rock and Alta Peak can be spotted upstream to the north. Continue down three switchbacks to smooth, polished flat rocks at the large Indian Head Pool. Rock steps lead to the various terraces and the water's edge. There are additional smaller pools upstream. A service bridge crossing the river can be seen downstream at a water gaging station. After exploring along the river, return along the same trail.

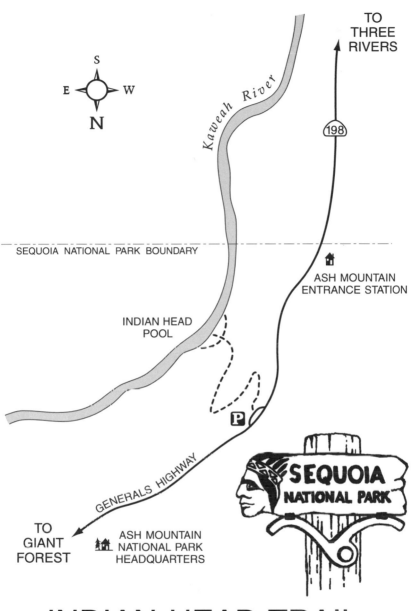

S
E W
N

Kaweah River

TO
THREE
RIVERS

(198)

SEQUOIA NATIONAL PARK BOUNDARY

ASH MOUNTAIN
ENTRANCE STATION

INDIAN HEAD
POOL

P

GENERALS HIGHWAY

TO
GIANT
FOREST

ASH MOUNTAIN
NATIONAL PARK
HEADQUARTERS

SEQUOIA
NATIONAL PARK

INDIAN HEAD TRAIL
TO
KAWEAH RIVER

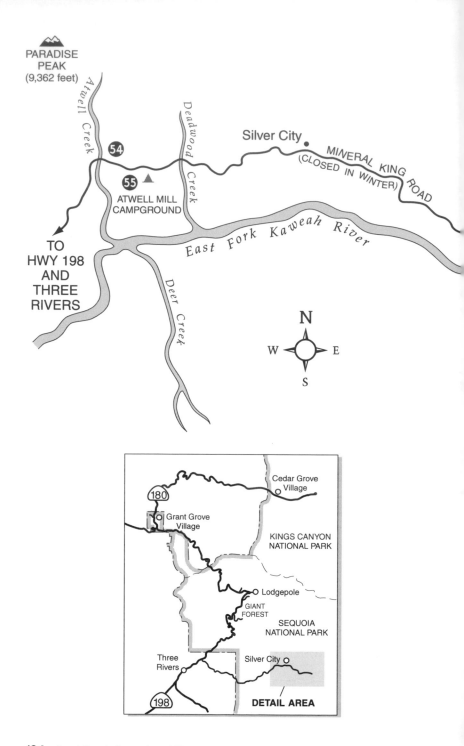

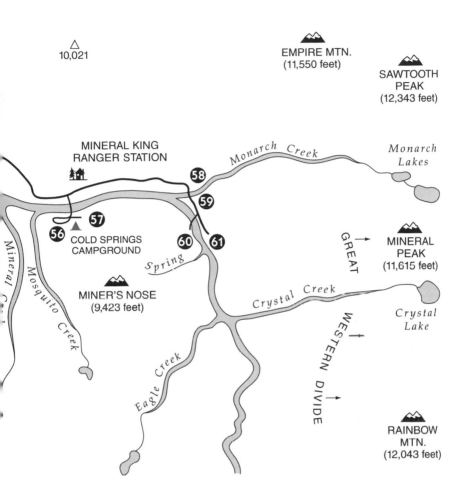

△
10,021

EMPIRE MTN.
(11,550 feet)

SAWTOOTH
PEAK
(12,343 feet)

MINERAL KING
RANGER STATION

Monarch Creek

Monarch
Lakes

58

59

57

56

COLD SPRINGS
CAMPGROUND

60   61

Spring

GREAT

MINERAL
PEAK
(11,615 feet)

MINER'S NOSE
(9,423 feet)

Crystal Creek

Crystal
Lake

Mineral Creek

Mosquito Creek

Eagle Creek

WESTERN DIVIDE

RAINBOW
MTN.
(12,043 feet)

MINERAL KING
HIKES 54–61

Hike 54
Paradise Ridge Trail

Hiking distance: 2.2 miles round trip
Hiking time: 1 hour
Elevation gain: 700 feet
Maps: U.S.G.S. Silver City

Summary of hike: The Paradise Ridge Trail climbs up a shady, forested hillside through a dense grove of giant sequoias. Along the way are great views of the East Fork Kaweah River canyon and the Great Western Divide.

Driving directions: From the Ash Mountain entrance, drive 2 miles southwest on Highway 198 into Three Rivers to Mineral King Road and turn left. Continue 19.3 miles on the mostly paved, narrow winding road to the signed Atwell-Hockett parking area on the left (north). It is located 0.2 miles east of the Atwell Mill Campground.

From Silver City, drive 1.5 miles west to the signed Atwell-Hockett parking area on the right (north).

Hiking directions: From the parking area, walk 0.3 miles west on the Mineral King Road, passing the Atwell-Mill Campground on the left, to the signed trail on the right. Short steep switchbacks lead uphill under a canopy of incense cedar, white fir, sugar pine and ponderosa pine. Within a half mile the trail enters a grove of giants sequoias. The path crosses fern-lined Atwell Creek as long, sweeping switchbacks make an easier grade. At 1.1 mile the trail comes to a clearing with great views of the canyon. This is a good spot to turn around.

To hike further, the trail continues as more switchback lead up the mountain to additional overlooks and a few more sequoias. The path reaches Paradise Ridge at 3 miles.

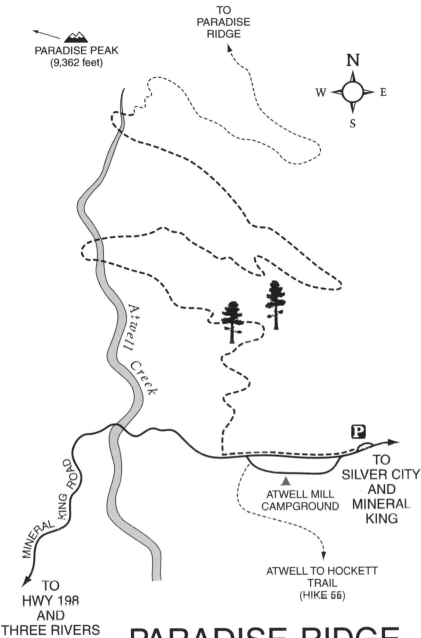

TO
PARADISE
RIDGE

PARADISE PEAK
(9,362 feet)

N
W ✦ E
S

Atwell Creek

MINERAL KING ROAD

P

TO
SILVER CITY
AND
MINERAL
KING

ATWELL MILL
CAMPGROUND

ATWELL TO HOCKETT
TRAIL
(HIKE 56)

TO
HWY 198
AND
THREE RIVERS

PARADISE RIDGE
TRAIL

Hike 55
Atwell—Hockett Trail
to East Fork Kaweah Falls

Hiking distance: 2.4 miles round trip
Hiking time: 1.5 hours
Elevation gain: 600 feet
Maps: U.S.G.S. Silver City

Summary of hike: This hike takes you through a dense ever-green forest with giant sequoias to a narrow, picturesque gorge. At the gorge is a bridge crossing the East Fork Kaweah River. Upstream from the bridge is a dynamic waterfall dropping over large granite boulders down a narrow chute to the pools below. Giant sequoias overlook the gorge from the hillside.

Driving directions: From the Ash Mountain entrance, drive 2 miles southwest on Highway 198 into Three Rivers to Mineral King Road and turn left. Continue 19.1 miles to the Atwell Mill Campground and turn right. Drive 0.2 miles to the signed trail-head parking area at the east end of the campground.

From Silver City, drive 1.7 miles west to the Atwell Mill Campground and turn left.

Hiking directions: From the parking area, walk back down the campground road to the signed trailhead by campsite 17. Take the wide path south past huge sequoia stumps, remnants from the logging days. Curve east, circling the hill into the dense evergreen forest. Descend along the south-facing slope of the canyon to Deadwood Creek, flowing through a ravine with a waterfall. Above the falls stands a beautiful giant sequoia. Rock hop across the creek and continue downhill. Look for bear and deer prints on the fine dirt path. At 1.2 miles, the trail crosses the East Fork bridge between the steep walls above the river. Upstream to the east is the waterfall with several pools below. After enjoying the gorge, return on the same path.

To hike further, the trail continues uphill through the small East Fork Grove of sequoias to Deer Creek at 2 miles.

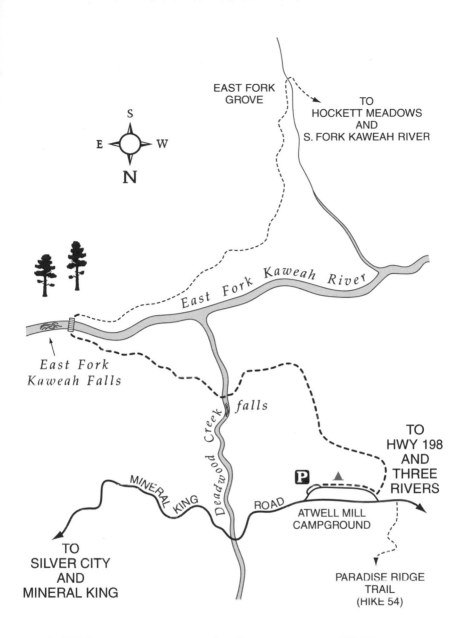

East Fork Grove

TO HOCKETT MEADOWS AND S. FORK KAWEAH RIVER

East Fork Kaweah River

East Fork Kaweah Falls

Deadwood Creek

falls

TO HWY 198 AND THREE RIVERS

P

MINERAL KING ROAD

ATWELL MILL CAMPGROUND

TO SILVER CITY AND MINERAL KING

PARADISE RIDGE TRAIL (HIKE 54)

ATWELL–HOCKETT TRAIL
TO
EAST FORK KAWEAH FALLS

Hike 56
Tar Gap Trail to Mineral Creek

Hiking distance: 2.5 miles round trip
Hiking time: 1.5 hours
Elevation gain: 600 feet
Maps: U.S.G.S. Mineral King
  Sequoia Natural History Association—Mineral King

Summary of hike: The Tar Gap Trail is one of two routes from Mineral King to the South Fork Kaweah River via Hockett Meadows. (The Atwell—Hockett Trail is the other route.) The trail is primarily a stock route, but the first few miles are perfect for a day hike. This hike begins in the Cold Springs Campground and crosses Mosquito Creek to Mineral Creek.

Driving directions: From the Ash Mountain entrance, drive 2 miles southeast on Highway 198 into Three Rivers to Mineral King Road and turn left. Continue 20.8 miles on the narrow and winding road to Silver City. From Silver City, drive 2.9 miles south to the signed Tar Gap parking area on the left, 0.3 miles past the Cold Springs Campground.

Hiking directions: From the parking area, walk 0.3 miles west on Mineral King Road to the Cold Springs Campground. Bear left, crossing the bridge over the East Fork Kaweah River on the campground road. Take the unpaved road 0.2 miles to the right, following the trail sign to Hockett Meadows by the walk-in campsites. Leave the road on the signed trail. Continuous switchbacks lead uphill through the shady red and white fir forest for a half mile to Mosquito Creek. (For a side trip, a narrow footpath detours along the east side of Mosquito Creek up to Mosquito Lake.) Rock hop over Mosquito Creek as the rocky path winds uphill to the lush vegetation at Mineral Creek. This is a good turnaround point.

To hike further, the trail levels out with small rises and dips, following the contours of the mountain. Choose your own turnaround spot.

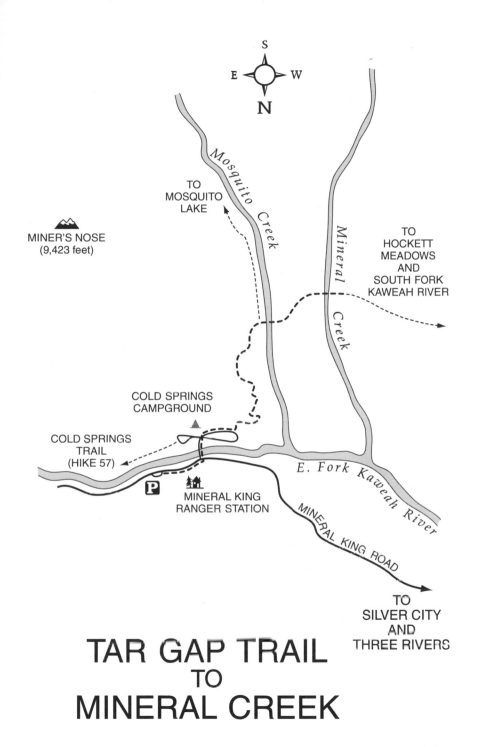

TAR GAP TRAIL
TO
MINERAL CREEK

Hike 57
Cold Springs Trail and Nature Loop

Hiking distance: 2.4 miles round trip
Hiking time: 1.5 hours
Elevation gain: 350 feet
Maps: U.S.G.S. Mineral King
Sequoia Natural History Association—Mineral King

Summary of hike: The Cold Springs Trail follows the East Fork Kaweah River up the glacially carved Mineral King valley. Towering mountain peaks surround the trail. Along the way is a nature loop with interpretive signposts about tree identification, plant life, abandoned mining activity and the geology of the area.

Driving directions: From the Ash Mountain entrance, drive 2 miles southeast on Highway 198 into Three Rivers to Mineral King Road and turn left. Continue 20.8 miles on the narrow and winding road to Silver City. From Silver City, drive 2.5 miles southeast to the signed Cold Springs Campground and turn right (south). Continue 0.1 mile, crossing a bridge over the East Fork Kaweah River, and turn left. Drive 0.1 mile to a small parking area by the signed trailhead on the left by campsite 6.

Hiking directions: Head up the canyon along the south side of the East Fork Kaweah River. At a quarter mile is a trail split, beginning the nature loop. Take the right fork, heading gently up the hillside and back down to the Cold Springs Trail. Take the right fork and continue upstream, parallel to the river. Pass several pools and cascades on the left. Switchbacks lead up into a shady evergreen grove, then quickly emerge from the shade to the dryer sagebrush slopes. Cross several wooden walkways over streams, then descend on rock steps along the edge of the cliffs above the river. The trail ends by a group of old cabins at the Eagle-Mosquito parking area. Return along the same trail, bearing right at the junction with the nature loop.

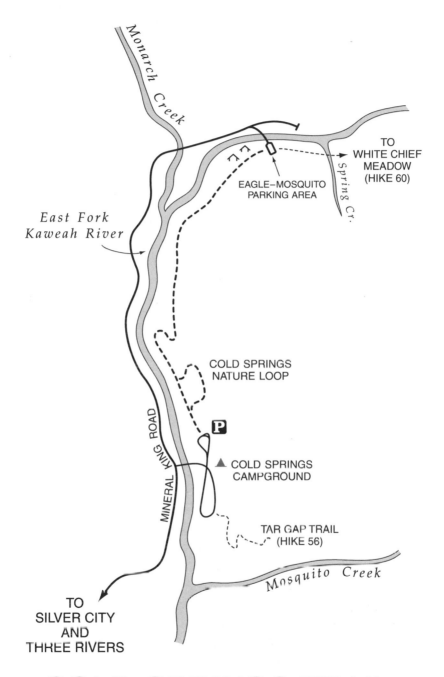

Monarch Creek

East Fork
Kaweah River

Spring Cr.

TO
WHITE CHIEF
MEADOW
(HIKE 60)

EAGLE–MOSQUITO
PARKING AREA

COLD SPRINGS
NATURE LOOP

MINERAL KING ROAD

P

▲ COLD SPRINGS
CAMPGROUND

TAR GAP TRAIL
(HIKE 56)

Mosquito Creek

TO
SILVER CITY
AND
THREE RIVERS

COLD SPRINGS TRAIL

Hike 58
Monarch Lakes Trail
to Groundhog Meadow

Hiking distance: 2 miles round trip
Hiking time: 1 hour
Elevation gain: 700 feet
Maps: U.S.G.S. Mineral King
Sequoia Natural History Association—Mineral King

Summary of hike: The hike to Groundhog Meadow follows the first portion of the Monarch Lakes Trail from the Sawtooth Trailhead. Groundhog Meadow is named for its abundance of marmots. The grassy meadow sits in a bowl surrounded by glaciated rocks alongside Monarch Creek. Along the trail is an overlook of Black Wolf Falls and views up and down the Mineral King valley.

Driving directions: From the Ash Mountain entrance, drive 2 miles southwest on Highway 198 into Three Rivers to Mineral King Road and turn left. Continue 20.8 miles on the narrow and winding road to Silver City. From Silver City, drive 3.5 miles east to the signed Sawtooth-Monarch parking area on the left (north) side of the road.

Hiking directions: Head up the exposed sagebrush and manzanita covered hillside on the rocky trail. Switchbacks lead steeply up the hillside to a view of Black Wolf Falls on Monarch Creek (Hike 59). At a quarter mile is a signed junction with the Timber Gap Trail. Stay to the right up the Monarch Creek drainage along the edge of Monarch Canyon, heading towards Monarch and Crystal Lakes. At one mile, the trail reaches Groundhog Meadow at the creek. This is the turnaround spot.

To hike further, the trail crosses the creek and steeply switchbacks up the forested hillside to Monarch Lake (4.2 miles from the trailhead) and Crystal Lake (4.5 miles from the trailhead). The Monarch and Crystal Lakes Trails are challenging, but the views are phenomenal.

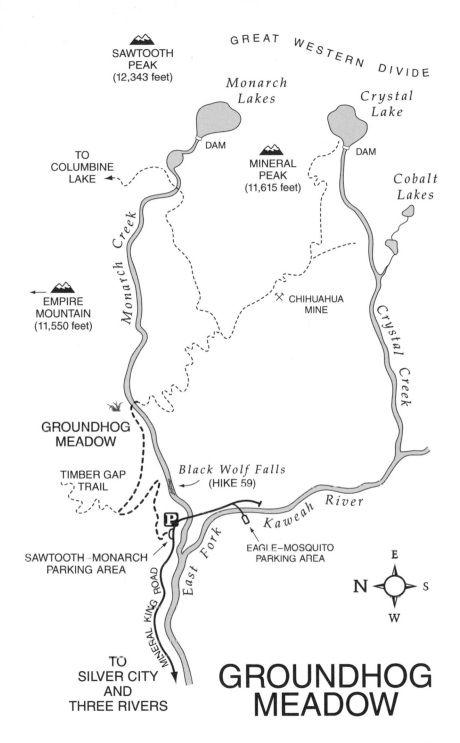

SAWTOOTH PEAK
(12,343 feet)

GREAT WESTERN DIVIDE

Monarch
Lakes

Crystal
Lake

DAM

TO
COLUMBINE
LAKE ←

MINERAL
PEAK
(11,615 feet)

DAM

Cobalt
Lakes

Monarch Creek

← EMPIRE
MOUNTAIN
(11,550 feet)

✕ CHIHUAHUA
MINE

Crystal Creek

GROUNDHOG
MEADOW

TIMBER GAP
TRAIL

Black Wolf Falls
(HIKE 59) ←

Kaweah River

East Fork

P

EAGLE–MOSQUITO
PARKING AREA

SAWTOOTH–MONARCH
PARKING AREA

MINERAL KING ROAD

TO
SILVER CITY
AND
THREE RIVERS

N W E S

GROUNDHOG MEADOW

Hike 59
Black Wolf Falls

Hiking distance: 0.5 miles round trip
Hiking time: 30 minutes
Elevation gain: 50 feet
Maps: U.S.G.S. Mineral King
   Sequoia Natural History Association—Mineral King

Summary of hike: Black Wolf Falls is a wide, 50-foot tall cataract on Monarch Creek. The waterfall cascades over beautiful multicolored rock into pools below. The clearly defined path to the falls is not a designated or maintained trail, but is short and easy to follow.

Driving directions: From the Ash Mountain entrance, drive 2 miles southwest on Highway 198 into Three Rivers to Mineral King Road and turn left. Continue 20.8 miles on the narrow and winding road to Silver City. From Silver City, drive 3.5 miles east to the signed Sawtooth-Monarch parking area on the left side of the road.

Hiking directions: Walk up canyon along Mineral King Road 0.1 mile, crossing over Monarch Creek. A short distance ahead is a rocky wash. Take the narrow footpath to the left along the north side of the wash, crossing the sagebrush-covered flat. The rocky trail crosses over to the south side of the wash. After crossing, bear left and climb steeply up the hill at the base of Empire Mountain. The rough path leads directly to Black Wolf Falls. At the base of the falls on the right side, look for a cave-like opening. It is an abandoned copper mine from the Black Wall Falls Mine, active in the 1870s.

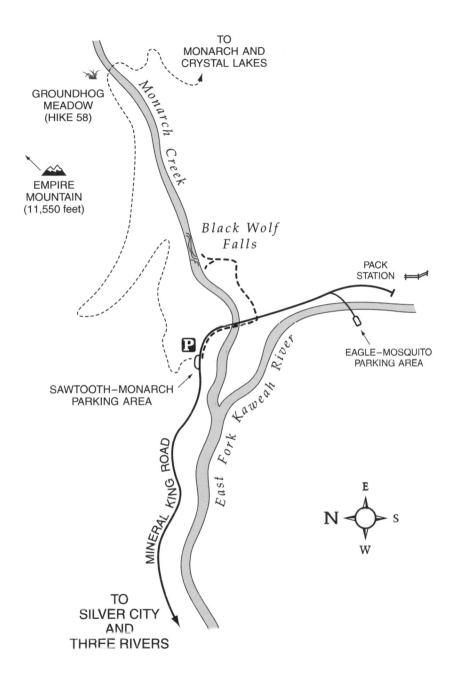

TO
MONARCH AND
CRYSTAL LAKES

GROUNDHOG
MEADOW
(HIKE 58)

Monarch Creek

EMPIRE
MOUNTAIN
(11,550 feet)

*Black Wolf
Falls*

PACK
STATION

SAWTOOTH–MONARCH
PARKING AREA

EAGLE–MOSQUITO
PARKING AREA

East Fork Kaweah River

MINERAL KING ROAD

N E S W

TO
SILVER CITY
AND
THREE RIVERS

BLACK WOLF FALLS

Hike 60
White Chief Trail to White Chief Meadow

Hiking distance: 4.5 miles round trip
Hiking time: 2.5 hours
Elevation gain: 1,350 feet
Maps: U.S.G.S. Mineral King
      Sequoia Natural History Association—Mineral King

Summary of hike: This hike leads up the west slope of Mineral King Valley to a beautiful subalpine meadow bordered by steep granite walls. The trail passes the Crabtree Cabin ruins, remnants of an 1870s bunkhouse for miners. Throughout the hike are phenomenal views of the surrounding majestic landscape.

Driving directions: Follow the driving directions for Hike 59 to Silver City. From Silver City, drive 3.8 miles east, bearing right at a fork, to the Eagle-Mosquito parking area at road's end.

Hiking directions: Head south past the trailhead map and the Honeymoon Cabin, built in the 1930s. Follow the west side of the East Fork Kaweah River up the valley. At 0.2 miles, cross a wooden bridge over cascading Spring Creek. Above the crossing is Tufa Falls, which can be heard but not seen. Tufa Falls can be seen from across the river on the Farewell Gap Trail (Hike 61). Traverse the valley's open west slope while steadily gaining elevation. Cascading Crystal Creek, the outlet stream from Crystal Lake, can be seen across the valley. At 0.9 miles, the trail crosses Eagle Creek. Steep switchbacks lead to a junction. The Eagle Lake Trail bears right. Stay on the White Chief Trail up the steep canyon wall parallel to White Chief Creek. The trail temporarily levels off, reaching John Crabtree's cabin on the right. Rock hop across the creek to White Chief Meadow. Meander through the meadow down to the creek. This is a great place to rest and take in the views.

To hike further, the trail leads up to White Chief Mine and White Chief Bowl, a 10,000-foot glacial cirque at the head of the canyon between White Chief Peak and Vandever Mountain.

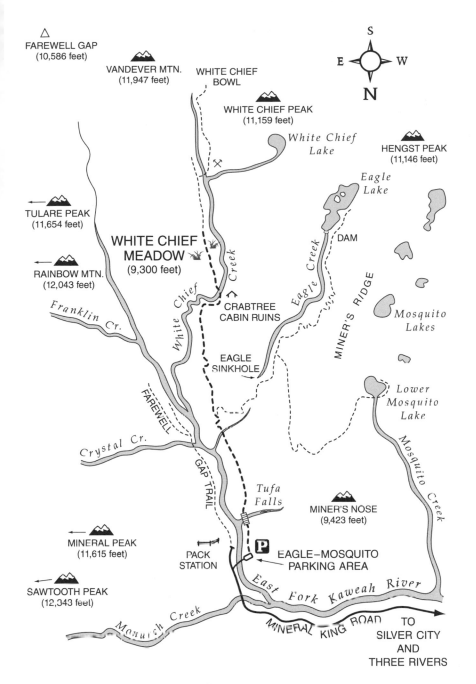

WHITE CHIEF TRAIL

Hike 61
Farewell Gap Trail
to Aspen Flats and Soda Springs

Hiking distance: 2.5 miles round trip
Hiking time: 1.5 hours
Elevation gain: 200 feet
Maps: U.S.G.S. Mineral King
        Sequoia Natural History Association—Mineral King

Summary of hike: The Farewell Gap Trail begins at the end of the road in Mineral King. The trail follows the East Fork Kaweah River up the stunning glacial valley in the shadows of 11,000-foot granite peaks. The path eventually climbs over Farewell Gap at the head of the valley, leaving Sequoia National Park. This hike stays on the valley floor and gains relatively little elevation. The trail passes two waterfalls to Aspen Flats, a grove of quaking aspen on the east edge of the river, and Soda Springs, a colorful, bubbling mineral spring along the river.

Driving directions: From the Ash Mountain entrance, drive 2 miles southwest into Three Rivers on Highway 198 to Mineral King Road and turn left. Continue 20.8 miles on the narrow and winding road to Silver City. From Silver City, drive 3.6 miles southeast to a road fork for the mule pack station. Park in the small pullouts along the right side of the road. If space is unavailable, drive 0.2 miles ahead on the right fork to the Eagle-Mosquito parking area at the end of the road.

Hiking directions: From the road fork, take the unpaved road on the left towards the Mineral King Pack Station. Beyond the corrals, continue south, parallel to the East Fork Kaweah River, up the wide valley floor. Across the river to the west is Spring Creek and the tumbling cascades of Tufa Falls. At 0.8 miles, the trail crosses Crystal Creek. After crossing, a short side path on the left leads to Crystal Falls, a 50-foot cataract. Return to the main trail and continue 100 yards to a trail split. Leave the Farewell Gap Trail, and take the right fork to Aspen Flats and

Soda Springs. This is a good turnaround spot. After relaxing by the river, return along the same trail.

To hike further, continue south as the trail begins to climb up the valley's east wall. Farewell Gap is 4.2 miles further.

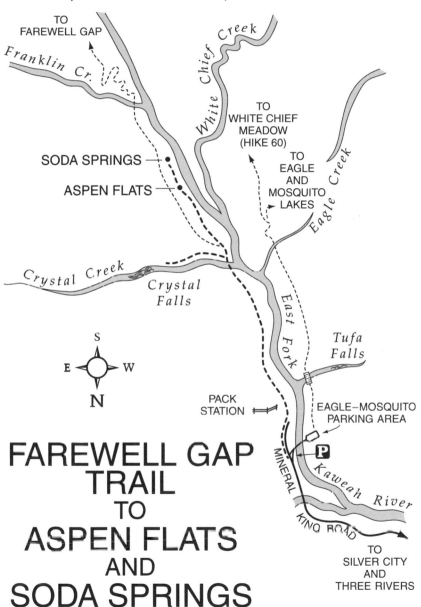

TO FAREWELL GAP

Franklin Cr.

White Chief Creek

TO WHITE CHIEF MEADOW (HIKE 60)

SODA SPRINGS

ASPEN FLATS

TO EAGLE AND MOSQUITO LAKES

Eagle Creek

Crystal Creek

Crystal Falls

East Fork

Tufa Falls

S
E ✦ W
N

PACK STATION

EAGLE–MOSQUITO PARKING AREA

FAREWELL GAP TRAIL TO ASPEN FLATS AND SODA SPRINGS

MINERAL KING ROAD

Kaweah River

TO SILVER CITY AND THREE RIVERS

DAY HIKE BOOKS

These books may be purchased at your local bookstore or outdoor shop. Or, order them direct from the distributor:

The Globe Pequot Press
246 Goose Lane • P.O. Box 480 • Guilford, CT 06437-0480
on the web: www.globe-pequot.com

800-243-0495

DAY HIKES ON THE
California Central Coast

71 GREAT HIKES
Robert Stone

DAY HIKES ON THE
California Southern Coast

100 GREAT HIKES
Robert Stone

DAY HIKES AROUND
Monterey & Carmel

77 GREAT HIKES
Robert Stone

DAY HIKES AROUND
Big Sur

80 GREAT HIKES
Robert Stone

DAY HIKES IN
SAN LUIS OBISPO COUNTY
CALIFORNIA

ROBERT STONE

DAY HIKES AROUND
Santa Barbara

82 GREAT HIKES
Robert Stone
2nd EDITION

DAY HIKES AROUND
Ventura County

82 GREAT HIKES
Robert Stone
2nd EDITION

LOS ANGELES TIMES BESTSELLER
DAY HIKES AROUND
Los Angeles
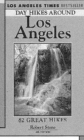
82 GREAT HIKES
Robert Stone
4th EDITION

DAY HIKES AROUND
Orange County
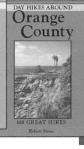
108 GREAT HIKES
Robert Stone

DAY HIKES AROUND
Sedona
ARIZONA

100 GREAT HIKES
Robert Stone

DAY HIKES IN
Yosemite
NATIONAL PARK

55 GREAT HIKES
Robert Stone
3rd EDITION

DAY HIKES IN
Sequoia & Kings Canyon
NATIONAL PARKS

Robert Stone

DAY HIKES ON
Oahu

37 GREAT HIKES
Robert Stone
3rd EDITION

DAY HIKES ON
Maui

55 GREAT HIKES
Robert Stone
3rd EDITION

DAY HIKES ON
Kauai

55 GREAT HIKES
Robert Stone
4th EDITION

DAY HIKES IN
Yellowstone
NATIONAL PARK

82 GREAT HIKES
Robert Stone
4th EDITION

DAY HIKES IN
Grand Teton
NATIONAL PARK

72 GREAT HIKES
Robert Stone
4th EDITION

DAY HIKES IN THE
BEARTOOTH MOUNTAINS

RED LODGE, MONTANA TO
YELLOWSTONE NATIONAL PARK
ROBERT STONE

DAY HIKES AROUND
BOZEMAN
MONTANA

INCLUDING THE GALLATIN
CANYON AND PARADISE VALLEY
ROBERT STONE

DAY HIKES AROUND
Missoula
MONTANA
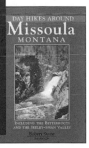
INCLUDING THE BITTERROOTS
AND THE SEELEY-SWAN VALLEY
Robert Stone

Notes

About the Author

For more than a decade, veteran hiker Robert Stone has been writer, photographer, and publisher of Day Hike Books. Robert has hiked every trail in the *Day Hike Book* series. With 21 hiking guides in the series, many in their second, third, and fourth editions, he has hiked thousands of miles of trails throughout the western United States and Hawaii. When Robert is not hiking, he researches, writes, and maps the hikes before returning to the trails. He is an active member of OWAC (Outdoor Writers Associaton of California). Robert spends summers in the Rocky Mountains of Montana and winters on the California Central Coast.